Healthy Treats and Super Snacks for Kids

PENNY WARNER

D1073040

CB

CONTEMPORARY
BOOKS

Library of Congress Cataloging-in-Publication Data

Warner, Penny.
    Healthy treats and super snacks for kids / Penny Warner.
       p.   cm.
    Includes index.
    ISBN 0-8092-3628-1
    1. Snack foods.   2. Quick and easy cookery.   I. Title.
TX740.W278   1994
641.5'3—dc20   94-28305
                                                    CIP

Design and illustrations by Georgene Sainati

Published by Contemporary Books
A division of NTC/Contemporary Publishing Group, Inc.
4255 West Touhy Avenue, Lincolnwood (Chicago), Illinois 60712-1975 U.S.A.
Copyright © 1994 by Penny Warner
All rights reserved. No part of this book may be reproduced, stored in a retrieval
system, or transmitted in any form or by any means, electronic, mechanical,
photocopying, recording, or otherwise, without the prior written permission of
NTC/Contemporary Publishing Group, Inc.
Printed in the United States of America
International Standard Book Number: 0-8092-3628-1
  890 DOC DOC 019876543

To Tom, my favorite gourmet,
and to Matt and Rebecca,
my former picky eaters

Contents

Acknowledgments

Many thanks to the students in my child development and special education courses at Chabot College, Contra Costa Community College, Diablo Valley College, and Ohlone College, for sharing their wonderful, creative, and tasty recipes:

Judy Baslee, Jamie Bell, Kathy Brazil, Judy Burhans, Gloria Devall, Caroline Duhamel, Holly Dunkin, Teri Dunkin, Linda Dutton, Cynthia Eborall, Elizabeth Figueroa, Vicki Fraser, Emily Grubbs, Shannon Gunner, Kim Gunsch, Tracy Harvey, Hilma Heaton, Catherine Johnson, Julie Johnson, Greg Kitajima, Zhila Larijani, Ashley Larson, Lala Manaserian, Lisa Mathews, Doug Mattson, Tina Nebiolini, Pilarchristina Newey, Diane Nixon, Elisa Onate, April Reprince, Jan Riley, Angeli Sala, Christina Sallas, Mary Segal, Renae Showman, Pam Skarlanic, Teresa Tang, Patty Tausheck, Lanel Taylor, Diana Tostada, Linda Thomas, Cathy Whiteneck, Jennifer Wilson, Jeanne Wood, Lynn Zug, and Pattie Zylka.

And a special thanks to Linda Gray and Lyle Steele for the opportunity to share these recipes.

Introduction

When was the last time your kids sat down at the table and said "Wow! That looks great! I can't wait to eat it all up!" If it's been a while, you probably have some picky eaters on your hands, just like I did when my children were little.

Those toothless bundles of joy were fairly easy to feed in the beginning. They wanted only one food—milk. But as my babies grew and it was time to introduce them to solid foods, I got my first hint of the battle that lay ahead. Pureed carrots came back at me in a spray of rejection. Globs of mashed peas were hurled Olympic distances like grenades. Baby liver pâté became airborne as it was flung from tiny silver spoons at a moving target—me. My maturing toddlers were learning expressions like "No!" and "Yuck!" and "Cookie!" and "Gross, Mom. I'm not eating this stuff on my plate."

War broke out—the evil food monster against the innocent offspring. Revolution was inevitable, and the battle lines were drawn. The color green was no longer allowed on the plate. Anything with texture was to be pounded, strangled, and ultimately crushed beyond recognition before it was surreptitiously fed to the dog. The call to dinner became a game of hide-and-seek. Morale was low, I was retreating further and further, and defeat loomed right around the kitchen corner.

When I realized I was becoming little more than a short-order cook, whipping up three to four different food choices for each child, each meal, each day, I knew I was losing the battle. The kids were getting pickier. They weren't getting enough good nutrition. And they would never learn to eat anything new if I kept serving the same old things every day. I had to do something—and I did.

I became devious.

I began smuggling nutritious foods into the old favorites— shredded zucchini in the hamburger, minced carrots in the pancake batter, wheat germ in the pizza dough. And they ate it!

I disguised nutritious foods with fancy packaging. I sailed tuna-filled bell pepper boats into their tummies. I made cute caterpillars out of vegetables and watched them crawl down the hatch. I shaped sandwiches into robots and hotcakes into zoo critters. And they gobbled them up!

I made the food attractive and inviting by using colored plates, champagne glasses, crazy straws, party sticks, and funny place mats. And not a crumb was left on the plate!

I gave everything a funny name, even if it was just the same old food they'd refused to eat before. I turned stuffed tomatoes into Red Balloons, spaghetti into Octopus Pasta, a rice dish into Pirate's Porridge, and an omelet into a UFO (Unidentified Frying Object). No one could resist my Volcanoes with Hot Lava on the Side, my Leprechaun's Shake, my Jungle Swamp Soup, or my Teddy Bear's Picnic. My daughter loved the cute names. My son loved the gross ones. And they couldn't get enough!

Finally, I distracted them. Instead of my trying to cajole, nag, threaten, or beg the kids to eat, we spent our time at the table discussing the day's events, telling jokes, playing games, being silly, and talking about the fun-to-eat meals and treats. They left the table happy and full of nutritious foods, and I left the table satisfied.

As an instructor of child development at four local colleges since 1986, I've learned from the experts—and the parents I teach—that most kids are picky eaters. They don't care if meals are good for them. It doesn't matter to them if the recipes are low in sugar, low in salt, low in fat, high in nutrition, and quick and easy to make and serve. All they want is good-tasting food. But I care.

As a result of the overwhelming success of my first two books, *Healthy Snacks for Kids* and *Super Snacks for Kids*, and inspired by my own two picky eaters, I've put together this all-new collection of delicious and fun-to-eat recipes for snacks, drinks, frozen treats, breakfasts, lunches, dinners, and desserts.

These recipes are quick and easy to make, nutritious and delicious to eat, and especially appealing to kids. Many of the recipes in this book were contributed by parents in my child development classes. They had the same concerns that I had and were eager to share recipes that were high in nutrition but were also foods that kids would eat.

I tried to strike a balance between what the kids want and what we want to serve them. These recipes are healthier than most packaged foods that kids might otherwise eat, without being strictly "health foods" which the kids won't touch. I've restricted the amounts of sugar, fat, and salt in all the recipes and deleted them completely whenever possible.

The food wars are over. *Healthy Treats and Super Snacks for Kids* will have your kids trying new foods, cleaning their plates, and asking for more. Don't be surprised if you hear "Wow, Mom [or Dad]! What a great snack [or meal]! It was yummy! Can I have more?" That's the sound of victory. Enjoy!

1
Sunshine Snacks

Whisker Doodles

These are tickly, just like Grandpa's whiskers, so be prepared for some giggles.

MAKES 1½–2 DOZEN

Melt peanut butter and margarine in a saucepan over low heat or in a bowl in the microwave, stirring to a smooth consistency. Stir in shredded wheat and drop by spoonfuls onto wax paper. Refrigerate until firm.

To store: These may be refrigerated in an airtight container for up to 1 week or frozen for up to 2 months.

1 cup peanut butter
   (creamy or chunky)
2 tablespoons
   margarine
2 cups crumbled
   shredded wheat

Nuts and Bolts

6 tablespoons
  margarine, melted
4 teaspoons
  Worcestershire
  sauce
¼ teaspoon garlic
  powder
¼ cup grated
  Parmesan cheese
6 cups mixed Chex,
  Crispix, and
  Cheerios or similar
  cereal
1 cup chopped
  pretzels
1 8-ounce jar dry-
  roasted peanuts,
  chopped

Sound crunchy? It is. Make it easy to eat by serving in sandwich bags, paper cups, or small bowls.

MAKES 8 CUPS

Heat oven to 250°F. Pour melted margarine into a 9" x 12" baking pan. Stir in Worcestershire sauce and garlic powder. Add remaining ingredients and mix until coated. Bake for 30–40 minutes, stirring occasionally. Pour out onto paper towels to cool slightly, then serve.

To store: These may be refrigerated in an airtight container for up to 1 week.

Zippy Popcorn

Add some zippety-doo-dah to the kids' favorite TV snack.

SERVES 4–6

Mix melted margarine with taco seasoning and blend well. Pop popcorn in oil (or in an air popper without oil) and pour into a large serving bowl. Stir in seasoned margarine mixture and toss lightly.

1/4 cup margarine, melted
1 tablespoon dry taco seasoning mix
2 tablespoons vegetable oil
1/2 cup popping corn

Mousetraps

1 cup flour
1 cup shredded
  cheddar cheese
½ cup (1 stick)
  margarine,
  softened
½ teaspoon
  Worcestershire
  sauce
1 green or red apple,
  cored and cut into
  thin wedges
  (optional)

If you're having a problem with little "mice" raiding the kitchen pantry, here's a "trap" that should stop them in their tracks.

MAKES 2 DOZEN

Heat oven to 350°F. Combine all ingredients except apple in a bowl and knead to form a ball of dough. Chill for 30 minutes. Shape into balls using 1 teaspoon dough. Place balls 2 inches apart on ungreased cookie sheets. Flatten with a fork and bake for 12 minutes. Serve warm or cooled.

For added fun, serve as flowers with each mousetrap surrounded by apple wedge petals.

To store: These may be refrigerated in an airtight container for up to 1 week.

Bugs in the Bed

This is a favorite snack in our family. Make up the filling ahead of time and keep in an airtight container in the refrigerator until serving time.

MAKES 16

Cut apples into quarters and remove core, leaving hollow for filling. Mix peanut butter, chopped peanuts, cereal, and raisins. Spoon into apple hollows.

4 green apples
1 cup chunky peanut butter
½ cup chopped peanuts (optional)
½ cup Rice Krispies
¼ cup raisins

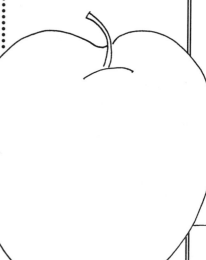

Ants in the Sand

2–4 graham crackers
Chocolate sprinkles

Kids love creepy stuff. They love to explore it, play with it, even eat it. Here's a funny snack that allows them to do all three. And it's soooo easy.

SERVES 1

Place graham crackers in a plastic sandwich bag and crush with a rolling pin or first crush the crackers on a cutting board and then pour into the bag. Add a few chocolate sprinkles to make ants, then seal the bag. Give to the kids to take outside and eat or let them pour it into a small bowl and eat at the table—using their fingers, of course.

Variations: Add raisins (call them beetles), red hots (ladybugs), or minicarob chips (spider eggs).

Fish in the River

These little fishies will swim right into children's mouths.

SERVES 1

Cut ends off celery and fill with cheese spread. Top with crackers and serve.

Variations: Use your imagination and try a variety of fillings and cracker shapes for fun, such as carrots, cucumbers, zucchini, or bananas as the holders and peanut butter, yogurt, liverwurst, or chicken salad spread as the filler, with raisins, nuts, grapes, or olives as the toppers.

2 celery ribs

¼ cup cream cheese or other cheese spread (tinted green if desired)

8 small fish-shaped crackers

Gooshy Gosh on a Ritz

1 very ripe banana,
   peeled
¼ cup creamy peanut
   butter
8 Ritz crackers (or
   other favorite
   crackers)

Here's what you can do with bananas you've had around the house a little too long. Kids love the name.

SERVES 1–2

Combine banana with peanut butter in a small bowl and mash with a fork or potato masher until smooth and spreadable. Spread on crackers and make them into sandwiches or keep them open-faced. Serve immediately, or spread may turn brown (then you'll have to give it another name).

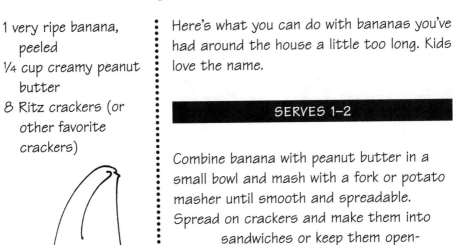

Cheezers

It looks like a cookie, but it tastes like a cheese snack. Let the kids decide what it is.

MAKES 18

Heat oven to 350°F. Spray a cookie sheet with vegetable oil spray. Scoop cheese spread into a bowl and mix with margarine until smooth and creamy. Add flour and mix until smooth. Roll into ½-inch balls and place on cookie sheet. Bake for 15 minutes, until lightly browned.

To store: These may be refrigerated in an airtight container for up to 1 week.

Vegetable oil spray
1 5-ounce jar processed cheese spread, such as Old English, American, or pimiento
½ cup (1 stick) margarine, softened
1 cup flour

Cheese Chips

1 teaspoon chili powder, Mexican seasoning, sesame seeds, or a combination
3 ounces Monterey Jack or Swiss cheese, cut into ½-inch cubes (about ½ cup)

A microwave cheese snack for the kids.

MAKES 3 DOZEN

Spread chili powder on a piece of wax paper. Turn cheese cubes in powder or seeds to coat on all sides. Set a 12-inch square of cooking parchment or brown paper bag in the microwave. Arrange 3 cubes about 2 inches apart on the paper. Cook on full power, turning paper several times, until cheese melts, bubbles, and turns slightly darker in color, about 1–2 minutes. Let stand until cool and firm, about 2 minutes. Peel off paper. To make more, wipe off parchment with paper towel and add 3 more coated cheese cubes.

Lizard Skins

What do you mean, your kids won't eat anything green? They'll love these Lizard Skins, which are just the right color green for a kid.

MAKES 16

Heat peanut butter with marshmallows in a large saucepan over low heat until melted (or melt in a large bowl in the microwave). Add green food coloring and mix in. Pour in cereal and stir quickly. Spray an 8-inch square pan with vegetable oil spray, then pour contents into the pan. Allow to cool in the refrigerator, then cut into long thin strips, about 1" × 4". Cut each raisin in half and stick on one end of each strip to make the lizard's eyes.

½ cup peanut butter (creamy or chunky)
1 12-ounce package marshmallows
2–4 drops green food coloring
4 cups Rice Krispies, Cheerios, or Corn Flakes cereal
Vegetable oil spray
16 raisins

Emeralds from Oz

1 green apple, cored and cut into small pieces
1 celery rib, chopped
1 small bunch grapes, each grape cut in half
2 tablespoons raisins, chopped nuts, and/or seeds (optional)
1 tablespoon honey
2–3 tablespoons mayonnaise

You still think the kids won't eat anything green? It's easy serving green, as long as you know how to put it together.

SERVES 2

Place apple, celery, and halved grapes in a bowl. Add raisins if desired. Stir in honey and mayonnaise and mix well. Spoon into individual bowls.

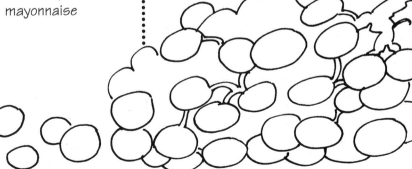

Bubble Balls

Watch out! These Bubble Balls will pop into the mouths of your kids.

MAKES 1 DOZEN

Mash bananas with a fork. Mix in half the nuts and seeds. Add honey. Form into small balls and roll in remaining ground nuts or seeds. Keep covered in refrigerator until serving time.

Give your snacks and meals a funny new name. Who can resist a Pirate's Surprise, a Screamin' Santa, or Wiggle Worms? If your child has a favorite TV or animated character, name the dish after it. Or make some of the names kind of yucky. They love that gooey, icky stuff.

2 large, ripe bananas
1 cup ground nuts
   and seeds
1 tablespoon honey

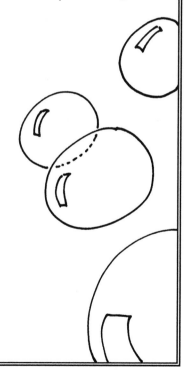

Snacksicles

3 cups miniature
   marshmallows
¼ cup margarine
¼ cup creamy peanut
   butter
3 cups Honey Nut &
   Oat or similar
   cereal
½ cup raisins
½ cup sunflower
   seeds
10 ice cream sticks

A snack-on-a-stick that's fun to eat!

MAKES 10

Heat marshmallows and margarine in a large saucepan over low heat, stirring constantly, until marshmallows are melted and smooth (or melt in a large bowl in the microwave). Blend in peanut butter, then add cereal, raisins, and sunflower seeds and stir well. Let stand 2 minutes. Form mixture into 10 2-inch balls. Insert sticks into balls and let stand about 30 minutes in refrigerator.

To store: These may be refrigerated in an airtight container for up to 1 week.

Snakeskin Sticks

These are fun to eat from a stick, but you can omit the sticks if you prefer and just serve them on a plate.

2 bananas
½ cup peanut butter
   (creamy or chunky)
1 cup Rice Krispies
4 ice cream sticks

MAKES 4

Cut bananas in half crosswise and insert ice cream sticks into cut ends, pushing stick halfway into banana. Spread peanut butter all over banana, then roll in Rice Krispies.

Get the kids involved in the cooking and they're more likely to become involved in the eating. Sometimes when they know what's in it, they're more likely to eat it, especially if they contributed to the outcome.

Gobbledygook

4 cups Cheerios or
  other toasted oat
  cereal
1 cup chopped shelled
  peanuts
1 cup raisins or dried
  pitted prunes or
  apricots, chopped
¼ cup margarine,
  melted
1 cup sunflower seeds
1 cup chopped
  pretzels

These treats cover all four food groups.
But the kids can't tell—they'll just think
they're four times better.

SERVES 6–8

Mix cereal, nuts, and raisins in a large bowl.
Pour melted margarine over cereal mixture
and toss lightly with fork until coated.
Sprinkle in seeds and pretzel bits and toss
again. (Or put the whole mixture into a
large plastic bag, seal, and shake well.)
Serve in sandwich bags or small bowls.

To store: These may be refrigerated in an
airtight container for up to 1 week.

Smiles and Giggles

You make the smiles; the treats provide the giggles. Add a tongue or a mustache for extra fun and flavor.

MAKES 4

Spread peanut butter on one side of each apple slice. Place four cheese cubes or tiny marshmallows on one apple slice, then top with another apple slice, peanut butter side down, and press closed to form a smile. If you want to be even more creative, add an apricot to make a tongue and/or shredded cheese along the top of the mouth to make a mustache.

1 red apple, cored and sliced into eighths
½ cup creamy peanut butter or cheese spread
16 small cubes of white cheese, such as Monterey Jack or mozzarella, or miniature marshmallows
1 dried apricot (optional)
Shredded cheddar cheese (optional)

Fantasy Island

1 cup peanut butter
(creamy or chunky)
1 celery rib from the
heart with a leafy
top
1 carrot, cut into 4
sticks
1 large cracker or
several small ones
1 apple, cored, cut
into wedges, and
the wedges cut in
half

Beware of circling sharks when you try to eat these treats. Substitute whatever dippers you wish to create an island, a raft, and a school of sharks.

SERVES 2

Place peanut butter in center of a plate and shape into a small mound. Place a leafy celery rib in center to make a tree. Arrange carrot sticks crosswise to make a square moored near the peanut butter island and top with a cracker to form a raft. Place apple wedge halves around the rest of the plate to form shark fins. Let kids dip veggies, fruit, and crackers into the peanut butter and gobble up Fantasy Island.

Teddy Bear Carousel

Take a snack break on the Teddy Bear Carousel. This is a fun treat to make with the kids.

MAKES 2

Cut apples crosswise into ¼-inch slices to form circles. Discard or eat top and bottom of apple. Spread two circles with peanut butter. Stick four toothpicks, equal distances apart, around the edge of one apple circle, peanut butter side up. Top with second apple circle, peanut butter side up, and secure to tops of toothpicks to form a carousel. Stand four Teddy Grahams in the peanut butter in between the toothpicks. Place a Gummi Bear in the center of the carousel roof. Repeat to make a second carousel. Serve (but be careful with toothpicks).

1 apple, cored
8 Teddy Grahams
2 Gummi Bears
¼ cup creamy peanut butter
8 toothpicks

Freckle-Faced Bears

Vegetable oil spray
1 10-ounce package
  refrigerator
  biscuits
¼ cup sesame or
  sunflower seeds
36 raisins

Even young children enjoy making their own Freckle-Faced Bears. But don't let them get too attached, or they won't eat their own creations!

MAKES 6

Heat oven to 400°F. Spray a cookie sheet with vegetable oil spray. Separate biscuits. Cut three biscuits into sixths for ears and noses and leave six biscuits whole for heads. Roll larger dough pieces into balls, roll in seeds, then flatten slightly on cookie sheet to form heads. Round three small pieces to form two ears and one nose for each head and roll in seeds. Press an ear on either side of each head near the top. Press a nose into the center of the head. Press a raisin into the center of both ears and two into the center of the nose. Add

two more above the nose to make eyes.
Bake for 8–10 minutes, until golden brown.

To store: These may be refrigerated in an
airtight container for up to 1 week or
frozen for up to 2 months.

You can smuggle good nutrition into
your snacks and meals in many
sneaky ways. You might try adding
shredded fruits or vegetables, wheat
germ, seeds, or other nutritious
additives to blender shakes, cheese
dips, cookie dough, pizza dough,
gelatin, hamburger, yogurt, noodle
casseroles, pancake batter, peanut
butter, scrambled eggs, egg salad,
tuna salad, and veggie dips.

Butterfly Bites

2 celery ribs
1 8-ounce jar cheddar
  cheese spread
8 large twist pretzels
Broken pretzel pieces
12 raisins

These adorable little critters will fly right into any open mouths in the vicinity.

MAKES 4

Cut celery ribs in half crosswise. Fill with cheese. Stick a twist pretzel onto both long edges of celery to form butterfly wings. Use broken pieces to make antennae at one end. Place 3 raisins down the middle of the cheese for decoration.

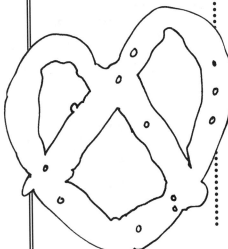

Cat's Eyes

These hypnotic treats will have them in a trance. They'll soon be chanting "More! More! More!"

MAKES 8

Spread peanut butter on crackers and top each with a slice of banana. Place a raisin in center of each banana to form a cat's eye and repeat for all banana-topped crackers.

½ cup peanut butter (creamy or chunky)
8 whole-wheat crackers
1 banana, peeled and cut into 8 round slices
8 raisins

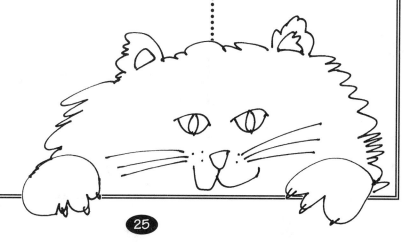

Stegosaurus Tasties

1 Ritz or other round
   cracker
2–3 tablespoons
   peanut butter
   (creamy or chunky)
   or cheese spread
1 cheese slice, cut
   into long triangular
   strips
3 raisins

Here's a creative snack you can turn into your favorite dinosaur. Or try another favorite animal, such as a turkey, a peacock, or a porcupine. All it takes is a little imagination.

MAKES 1

Cover cracker with peanut butter or cheese spread to make a body. Place cheese strips around edge, sticking up from top half of cracker. Add raisin eye at one side (side view) and two at bottom for feet.

Variations: To make a turkey, peacock, or porcupine, put raisins in the middle for eyes (front view), then make a small triangle for beak and add raisin feet.

Rudolph the Reindeer

You don't have to save Rudolph for the holidays; the kids will eat these year-round. If they prefer cats, just turn the antlers into whiskers.

MAKES 8

Spread peanut butter on bread slices and cut each slice into four triangles. Turn triangles so point is down, then place two raisins in center for eyes. Cut cherry in half and place one half at bottom point for nose. Break twist pretzels to make antlers and place at upper two corners.

Variation: Turn pretzels down near nose to make cats with whiskers.

¼ cup creamy peanut butter
2 slices whole-wheat bread
16 raisins
4 cherries
16 twist pretzels

Sailboats and Canoes

1 hard-cooked egg,
  peeled
1 tablespoon
  mayonnaise
1 teaspoon grated
  Parmesan cheese
1 celery rib
2 tablespoons cheese
  spread
1 cheese slice

These two sailing vessels will cruise right down the hatch.

MAKES 2 SAILBOATS AND 2 CANOES

Cut hard-cooked egg in half lengthwise. Remove yolk and mix with mayonnaise and Parmesan. Fill egg cavity with yolk mixture. Cut ends off celery rib, cut rib in half crosswise, and fill halves with cheese spread. Cut cheese slice into four triangles. Stick cheese triangles vertically into egg mixture and cheese spread to form sails.

Wagons

When it's time to rustle up some grub, these country wagons will do the job. If you need more speed, make them hot rods instead of wagons.

MAKES 4

Cut celery ribs crosswise into two pieces each, about 3 inches long. Push toothpicks through sides of celery to form "axles" for four wheels. Fill celery wagon with peanut butter, cheese, or dressing. Stick carrot wheels onto ends of toothpicks. Cover tips with raisins. Stick a toothpick into the end of the celery at a 45-degree angle to form wagon handle. Cover tip with raisin.

2 celery ribs
12 toothpicks
16 carrot rounds
½ cup peanut butter (creamy or chunky), cheese spread, or ranch dressing
20 raisins

Insects in Amber

1 tablespoon
   unflavored gelatin
1/4 cup water
1 1/2 cups apple juice
1/4 cup apple juice
   concentrate
Raisins or chocolate
   sprinkles

These not-quite-prehistoric finds may not be 50 zillion years old, but they sure are fun to discover. Let the little scientists examine their Insects in Amber before they send them off to extinction.

SERVES 4

Mix together gelatin and water and let stand 1 minute to soften. In a small saucepan, bring apple juice to a boil. Add juice to gelatin mixture and stir until gelatin is dissolved. Add juice concentrate. Pour mixture into an 8-inch square pan, sprinkle with raisins or chocolate sprinkles, and chill until firm. Cut into cubes or use dinosaur (or other) cookie cutters, then turn onto plate for discovery, examination, and refreshment.

Cookie Cutter Cheese Toasts

They look like cookies but taste like cheese toasts. Let the kids help you with these.

SERVES 1

Heat oven to 350°F or heat the broiler. Place bread slices on a cookie sheet and top each with a slice of cheese. Cut out shapes using cookie cutters, keeping the scraps. Place under broiler or in oven for a few minutes, until cheese is melted and bubbly. Serve the "cookies" and scraps and call the scraps "cookie chips."

2 slices bread
2 slices cheese
Cookie cutters

Wiggle Worms

A variety of fruit balls, squares, and chunks, such as grapes, cherries, cantaloupe, watermelon, other melon, pineapple, orange sections, banana, apricot, apple, pear, and strawberries
6 pretzel sticks
Chocolate sprinkles

These Wiggle Worms are fun to make, so let the kids help out.

SERVES 1

The fruit should be cut into chunks large enough to be threaded on a pretzel stick. Skewer three to four pieces onto each pretzel. Make a variety of worms using different fruit pieces, covering all of the pretzel except the end (tail). Use chocolate sprinkles to make eyes at the front of the worm and serve.

Slinkies

They're called Slinkies because they slither down your throat. Try different yogurt flavors and different cereals for variety.

SERVES 1

Layer ingredients in the glass in the order listed and serve with a spoon. Add other layers if desired, such as chopped nuts, coconut, seeds, another layer of yogurt, and so on.

1 tall glass or clear plastic cup
¼ cup strawberries or blueberries
1 6-ounce container vanilla yogurt
2 tablespoons carob chips or raisins
¼ cup Rice Krispies

Bananasauce

1 cup applesauce
½ to 1 banana, peeled
½ cup dry cereal,
  chopped nuts,
  raisins, or seeds
  (optional)

How about banana-flavored sauce as a change of pace from applesauce? It's easy to make, tastes good, and is good for your kids.

MAKES 1½–2 CUPS

Puree applesauce with banana in a blender. Serve as a smooth snack or mix in crunchy stuff if desired.

To store: This may be refrigerated in an airtight container for up to 1 week.

> Have a specific snack time each day instead of handouts all day long. Allow enough time before mealtimes so children will be hungry for the main course.

Confetti Cottage

Save your small milk and juice cartons for this fun-to-eat snack. You can make it as a surprise for the kids or have the kids make their own.

SERVES 1

Fill clean carton with your favorite drink (see Chapter 2 for ideas). Frost the carton with a layer of peanut butter or cream cheese. Decorate the cottage with a variety of crackers, pretzels, cereals, raisins, and seeds, covering it completely. Serve the Confetti Cottage with a straw and let the kids sip their drinks while they pick off all the goodies and gobble them up.

1 clean 8-ounce milk or juice carton
½ cup creamy peanut butter or softened cream cheese
A variety of crackers, pretzels, cereals, raisins, and seeds for decorating

Bunny Hoppers

¾ cup margarine
1¾ cups flour
½ cup packed light
   brown sugar
¼ cup honey
1 egg
1 teaspoon baking
   powder
½ teaspoon ground
   cinnamon
¾ teaspoon baking
   soda
1 teaspoon vanilla
   extract
2 cups rolled oats
1 cup finely shredded
   carrot
½ cup raisins

These Bunny Hoppers will jump right down the rabbit hole—your kids' mouths. But don't tell them what that crunchy nutritious ingredient is.

MAKES 4 DOZEN

Heat oven to 375°F. Using an electric mixer or a spoon, beat margarine until soft. Add flour, sugar, honey, egg, baking powder, cinnamon, baking soda, and vanilla. Beat well. Stir in oats, carrots, and raisins. Drop by rounded teaspoonfuls 2 inches apart onto an ungreased cookie sheet. Bake for 10–12 minutes, until golden.

To store: These may be refrigerated in an airtight container for up to 1 week or frozen for up to 2 months.

Monkey Bars

They'll go ape for these Monkey Bars. And these make great lunchbox stuffers.

MAKES 2 DOZEN

Heat oven to 350°F. Spray a 9″ × 13″ pan with vegetable oil spray. Stir together flour, oats, sugar, baking powder, cinnamon, baking soda, salt, and raisins in a large bowl. Add banana, milk, egg whites, and vanilla; beat until smooth. Spread batter into pan and bake until cake is golden brown, about 35–40 minutes. Serve warm or cool, cut into 2-inch squares.

To store: These may be refrigerated in an airtight container for up to 1 week or frozen for up to 2 months.

Vegetable oil spray
1/3 cup flour
1 cup quick-cooking oats
1/3 cup sugar or 1/4 cup honey
2 teaspoons baking powder
1 teaspoon ground cinnamon
1/2 teaspoon baking soda
Dash salt
1/2 cup raisins
1 cup mashed banana
1/4 cup skim milk
2 egg whites
1 teaspoon vanilla extract

Fruit Strips

1½ cups fruit puree, such as plum, apricot, peach, apple, nectarine, or strawberry

½ teaspoon lemon juice

Make your own fruit leather with the kids using this easy recipe. But make sure to start on a sunny day.

SERVES 3–4

Combine ingredients in a saucepan and bring to a boil over medium heat, stirring. When thick (the consistency of molasses), remove from heat and cool slightly. Cover a cookie sheet with plastic wrap and tape it to the pan at the edges. Pour mixture over plastic wrap and let it spread to approximately ¼ inch thick. Place in bright sunlight for 2–3 days, until no longer tacky. As an alternative in case of rainy weather, line a 15″ × 10″ × 1″ cookie sheet with foil and spray on vegetable oil spray. Spread the fruit mixture across the pan and place in a 300°F oven for 25 minutes. Then turn off the oven and let the fruit dry with the oven door closed for 8 hours (overnight). Tear into strips and serve.

To store: This may be refrigerated in an airtight container for up to 1 month or frozen for up to 3 months.

Spell-a-Pretzel

Vegetable oil spray
1 envelope active dry
   yeast
½ cup warm water
1 teaspoon honey
1 teaspoon salt
1⅓ cups flour
1 egg, beaten

Here's a smart snack. Create alphabet letters using pretzel dough and let the kids spell their names.

MAKES 6–10 SMALL ALPHABET LETTERS

Heat oven to 425°F. Spray a cookie sheet with vegetable oil spray. Dissolve yeast in warm water in a bowl. Add honey and salt and mix well. Add flour and knead dough until well mixed. Roll snakelike pieces and form into alphabet letters to make kids' names. Place on prepared cookie sheet and brush with beaten egg. Bake for 10 minutes. Serve with mustard if desired.

To store: These may be refrigerated in an airtight container for up to 1 week or frozen for up to 2 months.

Rainbow Ribbons

These colorful snacks-on-a-stick are almost too pretty to eat. But the kids seem to manage anyway.

Clean and cut fruit and place in separate bowls if you want the kids to make their own Rainbow Ribbons. Place fruit on skewers in order listed to make a rainbow.

Assorted fruit in the colors of the rainbow:
Red—watermelon balls, strawberries, or cherries
Orange—orange sections, cantaloupe balls, mango, or papaya
Yellow—pineapple cubes or banana slices
Green—green grapes, honeydew melon balls, or kiwifruit slices
Blue—large whole blueberries
Purple—purple grapes or cubed plums
Skewers

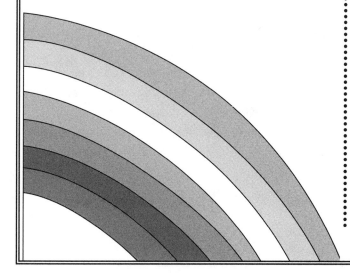

Snack Art

THE FOUNDATION
Celery ribs, carrot sticks, zucchini sticks or wheels, cucumber sticks or wheels, banana slices, orange sections, apple slices or wheels, pineapple slices, cantaloupe or melon slices or balls, or lettuce leaves

Why not turn your art project into a snack project at the same time? Start with clean hands, then let the budding artists create their own unique edible art. You provide the materials; they provide the creativity and imagination.

Offer the kids a variety of fruits and vegetables, prepared and placed on plates or in bowls, then give each child a plate to work on. Let them pick and choose what materials they want to use for their creation and offer plastic spoons, forks, and knives to use as tools. You might want to help the kids out with suggestions such as building cars and other forms of transportation, people, monsters, a space station, an under-the-sea panorama, or their names. Encourage them to name their finished work of art, then gobble it up.

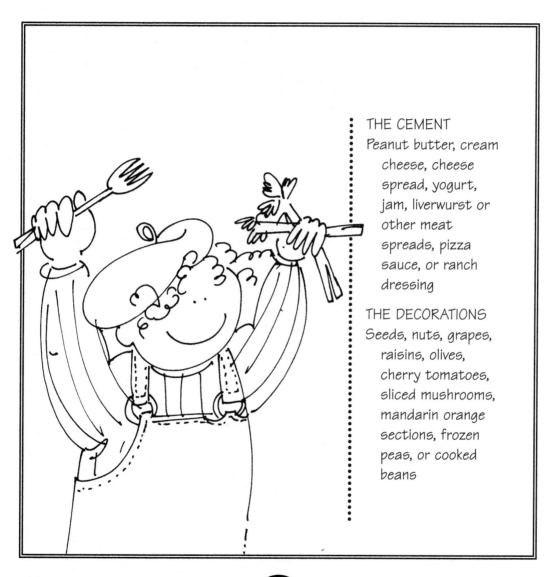

THE CEMENT
Peanut butter, cream cheese, cheese spread, yogurt, jam, liverwurst or other meat spreads, pizza sauce, or ranch dressing

THE DECORATIONS
Seeds, nuts, grapes, raisins, olives, cherry tomatoes, sliced mushrooms, mandarin orange sections, frozen peas, or cooked beans

Poppers

¼ cup cereal, such as Cheerios, Rice Krispies, or other crunchy cereal

¼ cup tiny crackers, broken pretzels, or chopped nuts

¼ cup dried fruit, such as raisins, chopped apricots, or chopped dates

1 plastic sandwich bag

1 cardboard tube, such as a toilet paper tube or paper towel tube cut in half

It really doesn't matter what you put inside these fun-to-eat treats as long as it's healthy. Use your imagination and fill them up with fun.

MAKES 1

Mix food ingredients together. Stuff plastic bag into paper tube and open up so it lines the tube inside. Fill with cereal, nuts, and fruit. Close plastic bag, then wrap tube in paper or cloth and tie off with ribbon or yarn. Give to kids and have them untie one end and pour out mixture a little bit at a time into their hands and eat!

To store: These may be stored for 2–3 weeks.

Wrapping paper, crepe
paper, or a scrap
of fabric approxi-
mately 6″ × 8″
2 strips of ribbon or
yarn, approximately
8″ long

Chocolate Spiders

1 12-ounce bag carob
  or chocolate chips
½ cup chopped
  peanuts
½ cup crispy chow
  mein noodles

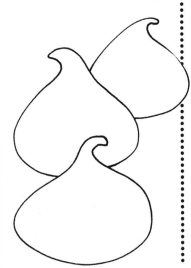

Oh, my! Swallow a spider that wiggles and jiggles and tickles inside.

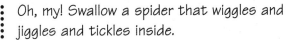

MAKES 1½–2 DOZEN

Melt chips in saucepan over low heat or in a bowl in the microwave. Remove pan from heat. Add peanuts and noodles and stir gently until thoroughly mixed together. Drop by tablespoonfuls onto a cookie sheet covered with wax paper and chill until firm.

To store: These may be refrigerated in an airtight container for up to 1 week or frozen for up to 2 months.

2
Delightful Drinks

Huckleberry Houndog

A meal in a glass that tastes great and fills the kids up until dinnertime.

SERVES 3

Whirl ingredients in a blender until smooth.

> **To lower sugar:** Watch for hidden sugar with names like dextrose, sucrose, glucose, syrup, molasses, honey, and corn sweeteners. Keep the sugar bowl off the table. Serve fresh fruits or juices instead of sugar treats and drinks. Sweeten foods with fruit. Use flavorings like cinnamon to enhance sweet flavors. When making recipes calling for sugar, reduce it by a third to half whenever possible.

1 cup skim milk
1 cup low-fat
   boysenberry yogurt
1 cup apple juice

Kids' Koffee

2 cups pineapple juice
3 cups apple cider or
   apple juice
2 cinnamon sticks
1 teaspoon whole
   cloves (optional)

Kids like to act like their parents, but what their parents eat or drink might not be good for them. This Kids' Koffee is nutritious, fun to make, and fun to drink from a coffee cup.

MAKES 5 CUPS

Pour pineapple juice and apple cider or juice into an electric coffee maker. Place cinnamon sticks and cloves in basket of coffee maker. Allow coffee maker to go through its regular cycle, then serve in coffee mugs. (You can heat this on the stove if you prefer, but the coffee maker method is fun for the kids to watch.)

Zapper

This drink has plenty of pizzazz, whether it's served warm or cold.

SERVES 3–4

Mix ingredients together, heat, and serve. Or serve it cold.

2 cups lemonade
½ cup orange juice
½ cup pineapple juice
⅓ cup grapefruit
   juice

Blackbeard's Ghost

2 cups skim milk
1 medium-size
   banana, peeled and
   sliced
1 teaspoon
   unsweetened carob
   or cocoa powder
2 teaspoons honey
   (optional)

A pirate's treasure—that's what this is, matey. The spirited flavors come together to make a thirst quencher powerful enough for any buccaneer.

MAKES 2 CUPS

Whirl all ingredients in a blender until smooth.

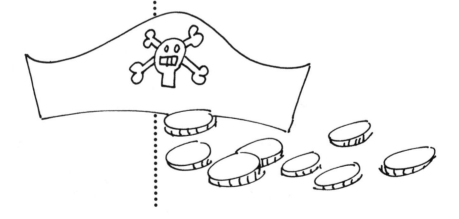

Earthquake Shake

You don't need an earthquake to give this drink a good shake. Just use a blender.

MAKES 3 CUPS

Mix all ingredients in a blender and whirl until ice cubes are crushed and drink is fluffy.

Talk about good nutrition as you eat. Ask questions, make up quizzes, play guessing games about the food and what's in it. Teach as you cook and serve so the kids grow up informed about good nutrition.

1 6-ounce can frozen juice, such as orange, pineapple, grape, or citrus punch
1 cup skim milk
1 cup water
1 teaspoon vanilla extract
1 teaspoon honey (optional)
1 tray ice cubes (about 1 dozen)

Witches' Brew

1 orange, peeled and
  cut into small
  pieces
1 16-ounce can
  apricot halves,
  chilled
½ cup cold skim milk
1 teaspoon vanilla
  extract

This pumpkin-colored drink goes well with
Halloween, but witches drink it year-round.

SERVES 4–5

Blend orange pieces and drained apricot
halves until smooth. Add milk and vanilla
and blend for 1 minute. Serve chilled.

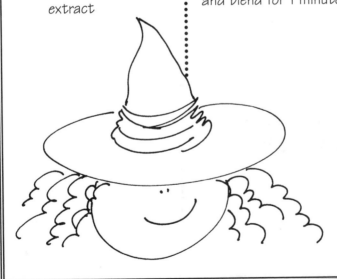

Purple Tickler

Don't worry. The kids won't turn purple.
They'll just be tickled pink!

SERVES 2

Combine ingredients in a blender and whirl
until smooth. Serve over ice.

> Present the food on cartoon plates,
> the drinks in champagne glasses,
> and offer a funny napkin to go with
> the meal or snack. Add a crazy
> straw or a fun-to-read place mat, or
> top the meal off with a paper
> umbrella or other table decoration.

1 8-ounce can fruit
   cocktail
1/4 cup grape juice

Orange Twister

1 8-ounce jar
  applesauce
1 cup orange juice

Have the kids guess the secret ingredient
that gives this orange drink a twist.

MAKES 2 CUPS

Combine ingredients in a blender and whirl
until smooth. Pour over ice.

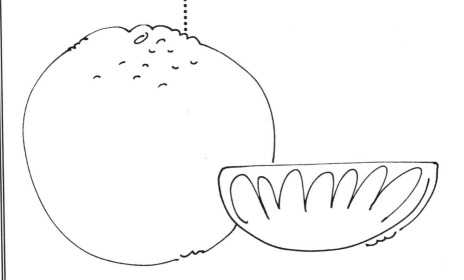

Tropical Storm

There's a tropical storm brewing—right there in your blender.

MAKES 2 CUPS

Whirl all ingredients except pineapple in a blender until smooth. Serve over ice, adding a pineapple garnish for fancy occasions.

1 banana, peeled and cut up
1 cup pineapple juice
¼ cup piña colada mix (nonalcoholic)
Pineapple chunks or slices for garnish (optional)

Chocolate Banana-Berry

1 pint strawberries
1 banana, peeled
¼ cup carob or
   chocolate syrup
2 cups skim milk

Three special tastes come together to make one wild new flavor. Better have refills on hand.

MAKES 4 CUPS

Rinse, hull, and slice berries. Slice banana. Place both in blender and whirl until smooth. Add syrup and milk and whirl again until well blended. Serve.

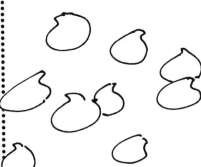

Dracula's Drink

Too gruesome for you? Then let the kids have it all—they'll love it.

Combine all ingredients in a blender and whirl until smooth. Serve in transparent cups, adding a licorice whip with both ends cut off as a straw.

½ cup plain low-fat yogurt
2 tablespoons water or juice
1 cup frozen strawberries
1 banana, peeled
1 tablespoon wheat germ
⅛ teaspoon ground cinnamon
¼ teaspoon lemon juice
2–3 licorice whips

Bunny Blizzard

1 cup skim milk
1 tablespoon honey
1 egg
¼ cup orange juice
¼ cup cooked
   carrots

A complete meal in a glass, just the way your wascally wabbits will like it.

SERVES 2

Heat milk and honey to nearly boiling in a small saucepan over medium heat. Beat egg with a wire whisk. Add to hot milk in a slow stream, beating constantly with whisk. Remove from heat and chill. When cold, pour into a blender, add orange juice and cooked carrots, and whirl until smooth.

Bossie the Grape

Our version of an old favorite, the Purple Cow.

1½ cups skim milk
½ cup grape juice
1 banana, peeled and
    sliced

SERVES 2

Place all ingredients in a blender and whirl until smooth.

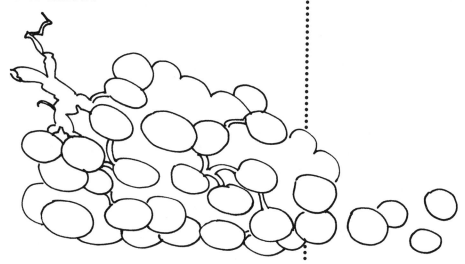

The Big Raspberry

1 8-ounce container
  lemon low-fat
  yogurt
3/4 cup skim milk
1/2 cup frozen or fresh
  raspberries
1 tablespoon honey
  (optional)

High in calcium and big on flavor. Let's hear
it for the Big Raspberry.

SERVES 2–3

Place all ingredients in a blender and whirl
until smooth.

Frosty Fruit Sodas

Here's a mix-and-match collection of fruit-and-soda drinks that the kids will love. Serve them in tall soda glasses if you have them handy.

SERVES 1

Place frozen yogurt at the bottom of a tall glass. Mix frozen fruit juice concentrate with carbonated beverage and pour into glass over frozen yogurt. Serve with a straw and a spoon.

1–2 scoops vanilla or fruit-flavored nonfat frozen yogurt

2 tablespoons frozen fruit drink concentrate: grape juice, lemonade, limeade, orange juice, pineapple juice, or pineapple-orange juice

3/4 cup sugar-free carbonated beverage, such as diet 7UP, diet Sprite, ginger ale, or club soda

Fruit Fizzy

3 cups apricot
  nectar
3 cups Sprite, 7UP, or
  club soda

Try a variety of fruits and fizzies or stick
with this one.

MAKES 6 CUPS

Mix fruit juice and soda together. Serve in
a chilled glass with a straw.

Raspberry Rain

Full of raspberries—just right for sipping on those rainy days—or any day.

SERVES 4–6

Combine raspberries and frozen yogurt in a blender. Stir in lemon juice and peppermint extract. Pour mixture into tall glasses and fill each with soda. Mix well and serve.

1 10-ounce package frozen raspberries, thawed
1 cup raspberry nonfat frozen yogurt
¼ cup lemon juice
Few drops peppermint extract (optional)
Sugar-free black raspberry soda

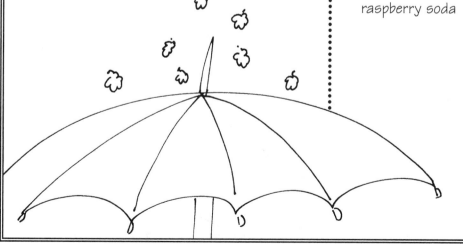

Summertime Splash

2 cups peeled and
   seeded watermelon
   chunks, chilled
½ cup white grape
   juice
½ cup club soda
2–3 ice cubes

Have you ever drunk a watermelon? Tell the kids that's what they're going to do when they down this Summertime Splash.

MAKES 3 CUPS

Combine watermelon with white grape juice in a blender and whirl until smooth. Pour into tall glass and stir in club soda. Add ice cubes and serve.

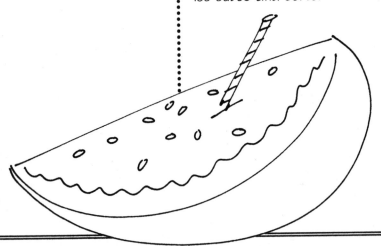

Eggless, Creamless Egg Cream

They call it an Egg Cream because the froth on top looks like beaten egg whites. But there are no eggs. There is no cream.

1/4 cup skim milk
2 tablespoons carob
   or chocolate syrup
3/4 cup club soda

SERVES 1

Pour milk into a tall glass. Add syrup and stir well. Slowly pour in cold club soda, stirring quickly until drink is frothy.

Keep the servings small and cut everything up into small bites. A child might be overwhelmed by piles of potatoes and stacks of pancakes. Cut down on the portions and let your child ask for more.

Tangerine Dream

2 tangerines
2 teaspoons lemon
  juice
1 12-ounce can
  cranberry or
  raspberry soda

This drink offers a naturally sweet taste and a change of pace from regular orange juice.

SERVES 1

Squeeze juice from tangerines into a glass, sifting off any seeds. Add lemon juice and soda and mix well.

Hurricane

Hold on to your glasses—there's a Hurricane brewing!

MAKES 3 CUPS

Pour all ingredients into a blender and whirl, like a Hurricane, until smooth and thick.

Hollow out fruits and vegetables that make good food holders and fill with fruit salads, sandwich fillers, pasta, and so on. Good fruits and vegetables to try: green peppers, pumpkin shells, orange shells, cantaloupes, celery stalks, cucumbers, and watermelon shells.

½ cup drained canned pineapple chunks
½ cup pineapple juice
2 drained canned peach halves, diced
1 cup vanilla or plain low-fat yogurt
1 cup skim milk

Mermaid Milk Shake

1 cup skim milk
½ cup chopped fresh
　or frozen then
　thawed
　strawberries
½ cup orange juice
1 6-ounce container
　low-fat strawberry
　yogurt

Here's what they drink down under—the sea, that is.

MAKES 3 CUPS

Combine all ingredients in a blender and whirl until smooth. Serve with a paper umbrella or a paper flower for fun.

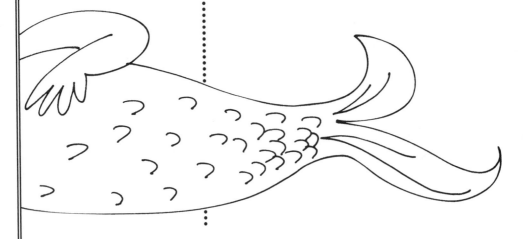

Houdini's Secret Slush

The kids are going to want to know the secret of Houdini's Secret Slush. Just tell them it's magical the way this smoothy disappears. (You don't have to mention the magical ingredients that make it such a nutritious drink.)

MAKES 2 CUPS

Whirl ingredients in a blender and serve cold to your waiting magicians so they can make it disappear.

1 8-ounce container vanilla low-fat yogurt
1 cup minced favorite fruit, such as strawberries, bananas, peaches, melon, or apricots
1 tablespoon wheat germ
1 teaspoon honey (optional)

Quicksand

2 cups skim milk
⅓ cup creamy peanut
  butter
½ banana, peeled and
  sliced
1 tablespoon honey
  (optional)
2 scoops vanilla
  nonfat frozen
  yogurt
6–8 ice cubes,
  crushed

Peanut butter and bananas are a kid-pleasing combination. Here's one they can sink their teeth into.

MAKES 3 CUPS

Place everything except the ice cubes in a blender. Blend on low speed for 1 minute, then add ice cubes and blend until smooth.

Lightning Bolt

A swallow of this power drink and the kids will think they've been struck by lightning.

MAKES 2 CUPS

Whirl all ingredients in a blender until smooth.

1 cup lemonade
½ cup lemon nonfat frozen yogurt
½ cup lemon-lime soda

Turkey Guzzler

3/4 cup skim milk
1 3-ounce package
  low-fat cream
  cheese, softened
2 cups vanilla nonfat
  frozen yogurt
1 8-ounce can jellied
  cranberry sauce
1 cup canned or
  frozen
  cranberries

No, there's no turkey in this Guzzler. But it's the perfect drink to serve the kids during the Thanksgiving holidays or anytime.

MAKES 5 CUPS

Pour milk into a blender, add cream cheese, and whirl until smooth. Add yogurt, sauce, and cranberries and blend until well mixed and smooth. Pour into glasses.

Peanut Butter and Jelly Shake

Why not put the kids' favorite sandwich makings together for a special drink?

SERVES 4

Combine all ingredients in a blender and whirl until smooth.

A sandwich doesn't always have to be packaged between two slices of bread. Try other ways of offering sandwich fillings by using ice cream cones, popovers, bagel slices, pita pockets, biscuits, crackers, cream puffs, dinner rolls, English muffins, hamburger buns, hot dog buns, raisin bread, toast, tortillas, or waffles.

2 cups apple juice
½ cup creamy peanut butter
1 tablespoon strawberry or other jelly
1 cup vanilla nonfat frozen yogurt
1 cup ice cubes

Pumpkin Punch

1 cup canned pumpkin
    puree
½ cup firmly packed
    brown sugar
¼ cup honey
1 teaspoon ground
    cinnamon
½ teaspoon ground
    nutmeg
½ cup orange juice
1 quart nonfat frozen
    vanilla yogurt

You don't have to wait for Halloween to serve this spicy shake.

SERVES 6

Combine ingredients in blender and whirl until smooth. Pour into hollowed-out orange shells to serve or ladle from a carved-out pumpkin.

Flash Flood

Here's a delicious, quick energy drink to wash down the snacks and revive those tired little bodies after a long day at school.

SERVES 2–3

Combine all ingredients in a blender and whirl until frothy.

2 cups orange juice
1 banana, peeled
1 egg white (optional)
4 ice cubes

3
Frosty Fun

Frozen Fireballs

Give the kids a frozen pop with a surprise inside. The spoons make them easy to eat.

MAKES 1 DOZEN

Pour juice into ice cube tray. Place 1 cherry or piece of fruit in each compartment. Place 1 spoon in each compartment. Freeze until firm and serve.

To store: These may be frozen for up to 2 months.

1 6-ounce can frozen orange juice, reconstituted
1 ice cube tray
12 maraschino cherries, small strawberries, or other small or cut-up fruit
12 2-inch plastic spoons (available at party supply stores) or ice cream sticks

Coco-Berry Bars

1 ¼-ounce envelope
    unflavored gelatin
1½ cups water
2 cups sliced fresh or
    thawed frozen
    strawberries
1 tablespoon lemon
    juice
½ teaspoon vanilla
    extract
1 cup cream of
    coconut
12 5-ounce paper
    cups
12 ice cream sticks

Make these pops in paper cups with ice cream sticks so the kids can peel and eat them.

MAKES 1 DOZEN

Soften gelatin in ½ cup of the water in a small saucepan for 5 minutes. Place over low heat and stir until dissolved. Cool for 10 minutes. Combine strawberries, lemon juice, and vanilla in a blender and whirl until smooth. Add gelatin, cream of coconut, and remaining 1 cup water. Blend until smooth. Pour into paper cups, cover with foil, and stick ice cream sticks into center. Freeze until firm.

To store: These may be frozen for up to 2 months.

Gator Pops

These aren't really made from alligators or any other reptile. They're made from Gatorade.

MAKES 1 DOZEN

Fill tray with Gatorade, insert a stick in each compartment, and freeze until firm.

To store: These may be frozen for up to 2 months.

1 32-ounce bottle Gatorade
1 ice cube tray
12 ice cream sticks

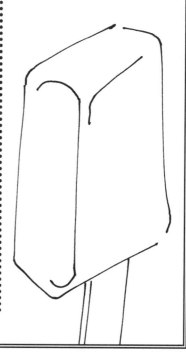

Frozen Universe

1 3-ounce package
   any flavor Jell-O
   (or use half of
   each of 2 packages
   and make 2-
   colored pops)
1 ice cube tray
1 8-ounce can fruit
   cocktail, drained
1 cup granola
1 16-ounce can juice
   of same flavor as
   Jell-O
12 ice cream sticks

We call this one the Frozen Universe because you can put practically anything under the sun into these pops.

MAKES 1 DOZEN

Prepare Jell-O according to package directions. Fill ice tray halfway with Jell-O and allow to chill until firm. Sprinkle with additions—fruit cocktail, granola, or other options. Pour in juice to fill remaining half, add ice cream sticks, and freeze until firm.

To store: These may be frozen for up to 2 months.

Variation: Instead of granola, you can also try coconut, seeds, chopped nuts, miniature marshmallows, or carob or chocolate chips.

Abracadabras

Magically easy and magically delicious. Can your kids guess the magic ingredients?

MAKES 1 DOZEN

Spoon applesauce into ice cube tray, add ice cream sticks, and freeze until firm.

To store: These may be frozen for up to 2 months.

1 16-ounce jar
   unsweetened
   applesauce
1 ice cube tray
12 ice cream sticks

Chilly Cherrysicles

3 cups cherry or
  berry low-fat
  yogurt
1 cup cherry or grape
  juice
½ cup frozen cherries
  or berries
1 teaspoon vanilla
  extract
6–8 paper cups
6–8 ice cream sticks

Chilly Cherrysicles are fun to eat during the holidays, but you can serve them anytime to your kids to make it feel like Christmas.

MAKES 6–8

Process all ingredients except cups and sticks in a blender until smooth. Pour into cups, insert ice cream sticks, and freeze until firm. Peel off paper cup to eat.

To store: These may be frozen for up to 2 months.

Snowflakes

Be sure to catch this mixture while it's at the mushy-firm stage so you can turn it into perfect little Snowflakes.

SERVES 8

Combine water with pineapple and lemon juices. Pour into an 8-inch square pan. Freeze until mushy-firm, like soft ice crystals. (If it freezes too solid, break up with spoon, put in a bowl, and beat with an electric mixer until ice crystals are broken up but not liquid.) Chip into small paper cups and serve with a spoon.

To store: These may be frozen for up to 2 months.

2 cups water
1 6-ounce can frozen pineapple juice concentrate, thawed
1 tablespoon lemon juice

Strawberry Snow

1 quart fresh or
frozen strawberries
1½ teaspoons lemon
juice
1 tablespoon honey
(optional)

Strawberry Snow is fun to eat because the snowy crystals melt in your mouth like magic.

SERVES 4

Place all ingredients in a blender and whirl until smooth. Pour into a shallow pan, cover, and freeze until firm. Remove from freezer and whirl in blender or with electric beaters until slushy. Pour into a bowl, cover, and freeze. Soften slightly before spooning into bowls.

To store: These may be frozen for up to 2 months.

Purple Monkey

Full of good nutrition, but the kids will never know it. Ask them if they can figure out why it's called a Purple Monkey.

SERVES 4

If you're using fresh berries, freeze them until firm. Place cottage cheese in a blender and whirl until smooth. Add frozen berries, bananas, and honey. Blend until smooth. Pour or scoop into individual bowls.

To store: These may be frozen for up to 2 months.

¾ cup fresh or frozen blueberries

1 cup low-fat cottage cheese

2 small bananas, peeled, sliced, and frozen

1 teaspoon honey (optional)

Frozen Sunshine

1 fresh papaya (about
   1 pound), peeled,
   seeded, and cut up,
   or 2 15-ounce cans
   mango slices,
   drained
2 tablespoons lemon
   juice
¼ cup honey
½ cup water
3–4 drops yellow
   food coloring
   (optional)

Frozen Sunshine tastes a little like sherbet. Can the kids guess what fruit you used?

SERVES 4

Combine all ingredients in a blender and whirl until smooth. Pour into a 9" x 5" x 3" loaf pan and freeze for about 4 hours, until almost firm. Transfer to a bowl and beat with an electric mixer until fluffy, about 2 minutes. Cover and freeze for 4–6 hours or until firm.

To store: These may be frozen for up to 2 months.

Jungle Juice Freeze

This frozen dessert seems to glow in the dark.

MAKES 2½ CUPS

Place pineapple chunks on a cookie sheet and freeze until firm. Place in a blender along with milk and reserved pineapple juice. Whirl until smooth. Serve immediately.

To store: This may be frozen for up to 2 months.

1 20-ounce can pineapple chunks in unsweetened juice, drained, ¾ cup juice reserved
¼ cup skim milk

Apple on a Stick

2 medium-size pears, peeled, cored, and cut up
1 apple, cored and chopped
½ cup apple juice
1 teaspoon lemon juice
6 5-ounce paper cups
6 ice cream sticks

Call the kids in for an apple on a stick and watch their surprise when you hand them a frozen applesicle. Have them guess what the other fruit flavor is.

MAKES 6

Combine pears, apple, apple juice, and lemon juice in a blender. Whirl until smooth. Pour into paper cups, add sticks, and freeze until firm. Let pops stand at room temperature for a few minutes before serving.

To store: These may be frozen for up to 2 months.

Pudding Pops

Your own Pudding Pops are better for the kids than the grocery store version.

MAKES 8

Prepare pudding according to package directions, using skim milk. Pour into paper cups, add sticks, and freeze until firm.

To store: These may be frozen for up to 2 months.

1 3-ounce package sugar-free chocolate or other flavor pudding mix

2 cups skim milk

8 5-ounce paper cups

8 ice cream sticks

Peanut Butter Pops

½ cup water
¼ cup honey
¼ cup creamy peanut
   butter
1 cup skim milk
8 5-ounce paper cups
8 ice cream sticks

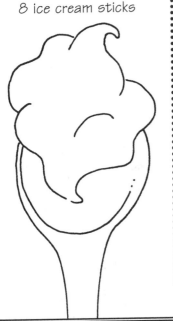

Frozen peanut butter? The kids will think you're crazy—until they taste these yummy treats!

MAKES 8

Boil water with honey in a small saucepan for 3 minutes, stirring until smooth. Remove from heat and stir in peanut butter. Stir in milk. Pour into cups, add sticks, and freeze until firm.

To store: These may be frozen for up to 2 months.

Cinnasicles

Dates provide a naturally sweet taste and are a good source of potassium.

MAKES 2

Whirl yogurt, cinnamon, and dates in a blender until smooth. Pour into paper cups, add sticks, and freeze.

To store: These may be frozen for up to 2 months.

½ cup plain low-fat yogurt
1 teaspoon ground cinnamon
½ cup chopped pitted dates
2 5-ounce paper cups
2 ice cream sticks

Lemon Freeze

1 ¼-ounce envelope
   unflavored gelatin
¼ cup boiling water
2 cups lemonade
2 egg whites

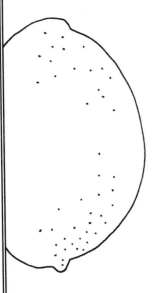

An icy treat for a hot day.

SERVES 4

Dissolve gelatin in boiling water. Add lemonade and chill until thickened. Add egg whites and beat until fluffy and thick and doubled in volume. Pour into cups and chill until firm, about 2 hours. Serve with a spoon.

To store: These may be frozen for up to 2 months.

Fruit Fluff

A light and fluffy frozen dessert made from your favorite berries and fruit.

SERVES 8

Combine berries with juice and puree in a blender. Fold in whipped cream and freeze in bowl until half frozen (about 1 hour). Remove from freezer and whip with mixer until fluffy. Refreeze. Repeat one more time.

To store: These may be frozen for up to 2 months.

1 quart fresh blackberries, raspberries, or other berries
1½ cups apple juice, berry nectar, or orange juice
½ cup heavy cream, whipped

Banana Scream

3 bananas
2 tablespoons skim
   milk

A naturally sweet shiver that makes the kids scream for more.

SERVES 4

Peel bananas, cut in half crosswise, wrap in plastic wrap, and freeze until firm. Place in blender, add milk, and whirl just until blended and creamy. Serve in small paper cups with small plastic spoons.

To store: These may be frozen for up to 2 months.

Frozen Stalactites

So easy, so cool, so much fun to eat. But are they stalactites or stalagmites? Depends on how you hold them!

SERVES 2–4

Slice melon into pie-shaped wedges. Lay on cookie sheet covered with wax paper and freeze until firm. Serve with a paper towel so the kids can hold the rind and eat the melon without freezing their fingers.

1 large slice of watermelon, cantaloupe, or honeydew melon, about ¾ inch thick

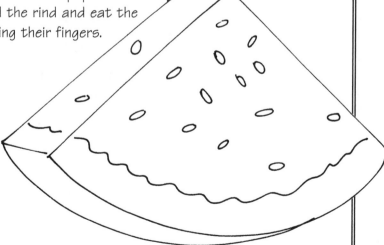

Peachy-Peachy

½ canned or fresh
   peach
½ cup peach nonfat
   frozen yogurt
3 tablespoons carob
   chips, melted
   (optional)

A double peach sundae, topped with a chocolatey taste.

SERVES 1

Place peach half in dessert dish. Fill with frozen yogurt. Pour melted carob chips over if desired.

To stick with good eating on the road, carry along finger foods and sandwich bags of trail mix that won't end up all over the car but will keep the kids occupied and satisfied. Good things to include: Cheerios, nuts, popcorn, trail mix, raisins, dried fruits, cheese cubes, crackers, fruit rolls, bread sticks, and cold pizza slices.

Twinkle Bars

These homemade ice cream sandwiches are higher in nutrition than the packaged variety.

MAKES 2

Soften yogurt and mix with peanut butter. Refreeze until firm. Spread on two cookies and top with remaining two cookies to make sandwiches. Store in plastic sandwich bags in the freezer until serving time.

½ cup vanilla low-fat frozen yogurt
¼ cup peanut butter (creamy or chunky)
4 large peanut butter or oatmeal cookies

Angel's Wings

1 banana
1 scoop vanilla nonfat
   frozen yogurt
1 tablespoon sugar-
   free whipped
   topping (optional)
¼ cup chopped nuts
   or sprinkles

These Angel's Wings are so pretty that you won't want to eat them—but that won't stop your little angels!

SERVES 1

Slice banana in half crosswise, then in half lengthwise, to form four long pieces. Place two on one side of a plate or dish and two on the other, side by side, to form wings. Place one scoop of frozen yogurt in center. Squirt or spoon out whipped topping on top of yogurt, then sprinkle with chopped nuts or sprinkles.

Blender Blizzard

Whip up a blizzard in the blender with this interesting combination of flavors.

Combine milk, syrup, and juice concentrate in a blender and whirl until smooth. Add frozen yogurt and whirl again until blended. Pour into cups and serve with straws and spoons.

1½ cups skim milk
2 tablespoons carob
  or chocolate syrup
½ 6-ounce can
  frozen pineapple
  juice concentrate
1 cup vanilla nonfat
  frozen yogurt

Sparklers

2 tablespoons skim
   milk
2 small scoops
   orange nonfat
   frozen yogurt
2 small scoops vanilla
   nonfat frozen
   yogurt
½ 12-ounce can
   grapefruit soda

This refreshing frozen drink gives a tingle
all the way down.

SERVES 1

Pour milk into a tall glass. Fill with
alternating scoops of orange and vanilla
yogurt. Pour grapefruit soda quickly into
glass and stir lightly. Serve immediately.

104

Leprechaun's Shake

Here's a drink that matches your St. Patrick's Day plans perfectly. But you can drink our Leprechaun's Shake year-round.

SERVES 1

Pour all ingredients into a blender and whirl until smooth and green. Serve with a shamrock.

1 cup skim milk
2 scoops vanilla nonfat frozen yogurt
1 teaspoon peppermint extract
2–3 drops green food coloring

Marbles

2 8-ounce cartons
   strawberry nonfat
   yogurt
1 cup sliced fresh
   strawberries
1 tablespoon honey
   (optional)
8 5-ounce paper cups
1 banana, cut into
   rounds and then
   rounds cut into
   quarters
8 ice cream sticks

Discovering the frozen "marbles" in these frosty pops is almost as fun as gobbling them down.

MAKES 8

In a blender, combine yogurt, strawberries, and honey and whirl until smooth. Pour into paper cups. Roll banana quarters into balls and drop into yogurt mixture. Add sticks and freeze until firm.

Tahiti Tingler

Having a tropical heat wave? Here's the way to cool down.

SERVES 4

Place all ingredients in a blender and whirl until icy. Pour into cups and serve with straws and spoons.

When a child won't try a new food, try these approaches: Grow it in your garden. Let him pick it from the grocery shelf. Serve it in several different ways. Offer it with dips, toppings, or mixed with other foods. Model the behavior. Offer alternatives. Don't become obsessed about a few unpopular foods.

1 32-ounce container pineapple, coconut, or vanilla nonfat yogurt

1 12-ounce can grape juice concentrate, thawed until slushy

1 cup pineapple chunks

2 cups ice

Snappy Sandwiches

1 pint mint chip or
    other flavor nonfat
    frozen yogurt
8 large sugar-free
    gingersnaps or
    other sugar-free
    cookies (available in
    health food
    sections of grocery
    stores)
3 tablespoons
    chopped nuts

You can use a number of different combinations to make your own sandwiches. These are snappy because they're made with gingersnaps.

MAKES 4

Line a 15" × 10" cookie sheet with plastic wrap. Place frozen yogurt in pan and cover with more plastic wrap. Knead flat slightly using your hands, then roll with a rolling pin into a 4-inch circle 1 inch thick. Freeze until firm, about 1 hour. Dip a 2-inch round cookie cutter in hot water, then cut out ice cream circles. Lift out with spatula and sandwich between 2 large cookies. Roll edges in chopped nuts, then refreeze until firm.

Variation: Cut ice cream into squares and sandwich between graham crackers.

Arctic Pie

An after-school special to share with the whole neighborhood on a hot day. Make an extra for dessert tonight.

SERVES 8

Make a pastry shell by combining oats, flour, coconut, and oil. Gradually add just enough fruit juice to make a soft dough. Press into a 9-inch pie pan sprayed with vegetable oil spray. Bake at 375°F for 15 minutes, until lightly browned. Chill. Whirl concentrated fruit juice and egg yolks in a blender. Add yogurt and whirl until just mixed. Pour into an 8-inch square pan and freeze until slushy. Beat egg whites until stiff. Combine partially frozen mixture with egg whites. Pour into piecrust and freeze. Allow to sit at room temperature for 15 minutes to soften before serving.

1 cup rolled oats
½ cup flour
¾ cup flaked coconut
5 tablespoons vegetable oil
2 tablespoons fruit juice
Vegetable oil spray
1½ cups frozen fruit juice concentrate
2 eggs, separated
2 cups plain low-fat yogurt

Eskimo Sticks

4 bananas, peeled
½ cup granola
¼ cup unsweetened
  flaked coconut
  (available at health
  food stores)
¼ cup chopped
  peanuts
1 6-ounce package
  carob or chocolate
  chips
1 tablespoon
  margarine
8 ice cream sticks

Fresh from the frozen tundra, these Eskimo Sticks will keep the kids cool.

MAKES 8

Cut bananas in half crosswise and insert ice cream sticks into cut ends. Combine granola, coconut, and peanuts and set aside. Melt chips and margarine in a saucepan over low heat. Brush carob mixture on bananas, then roll them in granola mixture. Place on a pan lined with wax paper and freeze until firm. When frozen, wrap in plastic wrap or serve immediately.

To store: These may be frozen for up to 2 months.

4
Beaming Breakfasts

Moo, Oink, and Squeal Muffins

Low in sugar, high in oats and fruit, these muffins are a complete breakfast in a muffin cup.

MAKES 1 DOZEN

Heat oven to 400°F. Spray a 12-cup muffin tin with vegetable oil spray or line cups with paper liners. Combine oats, flour, cinnamon, baking powder, and baking soda in a bowl and mix well. Add remaining ingredients and mix just until moistened. Fill cups almost full. Bake for 20–25 minutes, until golden brown.

To store: These may be refrigerated in an airtight container for up to 1 week or frozen for up to 2 months.

Vegetable oil spray or paper liners
1½ cups oats
1¼ cups flour
¾ teaspoon ground cinnamon
1 teaspoon baking powder
¾ teaspoon baking soda
1 cup applesauce
½ cup skim milk
⅓ cup firmly packed light brown sugar
3 tablespoons vegetable oil
1 egg white

Mega-Mini-Muffins

Vegetable oil spray or
  mini paper liners
2½ cups flour
½ cup honey
3½ teaspoons baking
  powder
1 teaspoon salt
3 tablespoons
  vegetable oil
1¼ cups skim milk
1 egg
¼ cup minced nuts
¼ cup mashed
  banana
¼ cup grated carrot
¼ cup grated
  zucchini
¼ cup raisins

Mega because they're loaded with good stuff, mini because they're teeny tiny. Kids love to pop these mini-meals into their mouths.

MAKES 4 DOZEN

Heat oven to 350°F. Spray a 48-cup mini-muffin tin with vegetable oil spray or line cups with paper liners. Combine flour, honey, baking powder, salt, oil, milk, and egg in a bowl and mix well. Add remaining ingredients and stir until blended. Pour into muffin cups and bake for 10–15 minutes, until golden brown and a toothpick inserted in a muffin comes out clean.

To store: These may be refrigerated in an airtight container for up to 1 week or frozen for up to 2 months.

Pig Puffs

Little pig, little pig, what's to eat? Pig Puffs, Pig Puffs, a kid's favorite treat!

MAKES 12

Heat oven to 400°F. Spray a 12-cup muffin tin with vegetable oil spray. Prepare corn bread/muffin mix according to package directions. Add corn and crumbled bacon and mix well. Spoon into muffin cups and bake for 15–20 minutes, until a toothpick inserted in a muffin comes out clean.

To store: These may be refrigerated in an airtight container for up to 1 week or frozen for up to 2 months.

Vegetable oil spray
1 12-ounce package corn bread/muffin mix
1 12-ounce can whole-kernel corn, drained
12 slices bacon, cooked, drained, and crumbled

Apple Bobs

Vegetable oil spray or
  paper liners
1 egg
2 tablespoons
  vegetable oil
2 cups applesauce
2 cups flour
3/4 teaspoon baking
  soda
1½ teaspoons baking
  powder
1 teaspoon ground
  nutmeg
1½ teaspoons ground
  cinnamon
½ cup chopped
  pitted dates
  (optional)
½ cup chopped
  walnuts

For a breakfast on the run, try these Apple Bobs—so the kids won't be late for school.

MAKES 1 DOZEN

Heat oven to 350°F. Spray a 12-cup muffin tin with vegetable oil spray or line cups with paper liners. Combine egg, oil, and applesauce in a bowl. Add flour, baking soda, baking powder, nutmeg, and cinnamon and mix well. Stir in dates and walnuts. Pour into muffin cups and bake for 20–25 minutes until a toothpick inserted in a muffin comes out clean.

To store: These may be refrigerated in an airtight container for up to 1 week or frozen for up to 2 months.

Jam-in-the-Box

Quick, easy, and full of surprises!

MAKES 8

Heat oven to 400°F. Spray an 8-cup muffin tin with vegetable oil spray. Prepare biscuits according to package directions. Set each biscuit in a muffin cup. Poke a hole in the middle of each biscuit with a clean finger and fill with jam or jelly. Pinch opening closed to hide jam and bake according to package directions.

To store: These may be refrigerated in an airtight container for up to 1 week or frozen for up to 2 months.

Vegetable oil spray
1 8-ounce package refrigerator biscuits (8 biscuits)
¼ cup low-sugar jam or jelly

Little Piggies

1 10-ounce package
  refrigerator
  biscuits
Vegetable oil spray
Raisins

Let the kids help you make these Little Piggies, then serve with bacon for a "pig-out" breakfast.

MAKES 5

Divide up biscuits, allowing two biscuits per pig. Use one round biscuit for the face and place on a cookie sheet sprayed with vegetable oil spray. Divide other biscuit in half. Use one half to make the snout by rolling it into a ball and then pressing it flat and putting it in the center of the pig face. Divide the other half again, round into balls, press flat with thumbs, and place on either side of face for ears. Use raisins for eyes (and inside snout and ears if desired). Bake according to package directions, until golden brown.

To store: These may be refrigerated in an airtight container for up to 1 week or frozen for up to 2 months.

Pockets Full of Sunshine

1 10-ounce package
   refrigerator
   biscuits (10
   biscuits)
1 6-ounce package
   sliced Canadian
   bacon
5 slices Swiss cheese
1 egg, slightly beaten
Vegetable oil spray
2 tablespoons
   margarine
2 red apples, cored
   and sliced

A breakfast surprise full of good nutrition and lots of fun.

MAKES 5

Heat oven to 400°F. Roll each biscuit into a 4-inch circle. Press half of the circles with a fork to make a decoration. Divide bacon and cheese among the five undecorated circles, leaving a ½-inch border. Trim to fit as needed. Top with decorated biscuit rounds and press edges with fork to seal completely. Brush top with beaten egg. Bake on cookie sheet sprayed with vegetable oil spray 12 minutes, until golden brown. Meanwhile, melt margarine in skillet over medium heat and add apple slices. Cook, turning once, until golden, about 8 minutes. Top biscuits with apple slices.

Happy Face Breakfast

Serve this Happy Face Breakfast and start the day with a smile.

SERVES 1

Heat a small skillet sprayed with vegetable oil spray. Gently break two eggs into pan, side by side, to form large eyes. Cook sunny-side up to desired firmness. Toast raisin bread and place on plate. Place slice of cheese on bread. Gently place eggs on top of bread and cheese. Place orange wedge at bottom to form smiling mouth. Use remaining orange wedges to create ears or funny hair, or just to border the bread.

Vegetable oil spray
2 eggs
1 slice raisin bread
1 slice cheese
1 orange, sliced into eighths

Freckle Popovers

Vegetable oil spray
3 eggs
1 cup skim milk
1 cup flour
Dash salt
½ cup small
  blueberries, rinsed
  and drained

Blueberries give these tasty breakfast treats their freckles, but tell the kids they're not contagious; only the good nutrition is. Check the variations for other popover flavors.

MAKES 8–10

Do not preheat oven. Spray 8–10 muffin cups with vegetable oil spray. Break eggs into a bowl and beat gently. Add milk, flour, and salt and stir until just mixed. Stir in blueberries. Pour into muffin cups. Bake at 400 degrees for 30 minutes, until golden brown and puffy. Serve warm with jelly, honey, margarine, syrup, or fruit.

Variations: Instead of blueberries, try 8 slices cooked bacon, crumbled; ⅓ cup cheddar cheese, shredded; 3 teaspoons ground cinnamon; 2 teaspoons garlic or onion powder; or 2 tablespoons Parmesan cheese, grated.

Cut up foods and rearrange them on the plates to make funny designs, crazy animals, or the letters in your child's name. Sandwiches can be cut into shapes so the kids can create their own spaceships, monsters, or buildings. And cut-up vegetables and fruits can be added for detail. Cut wings for your apple slices, add carrot tops to hard-cooked eggs, and use raisins to make faces on your foods.

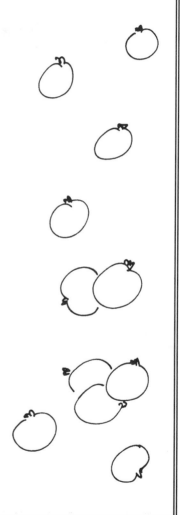

Crispy Critter

¼ cup skim milk
2–3 drops each red, blue, green, and yellow (or other colors) food coloring, the darker, the better
2 slices whole-wheat bread
2 clean paintbrushes

Let the kids be creative with their morning toast. Just give them the "paints" and let them make a funny face, a monster mask, or a creepy critter. Then toast and eat.

MAKES 2 SLICES

Pour 1 tablespoon milk into each of four small cups. Drop food coloring into each cup to make four different colors. Let the kids dip their clean brushes into the food coloring mixture and lightly paint a face or critter onto a slice of bread. Then toast bread, butter lightly, and serve.

Variation: Tint small amounts of margarine with food color, then have the kids paint the colors onto bread, toast, and eat.

Bull's-Eye

You can be creative with your center design and vary it each time you make a Bull's-Eye.

MAKES 1

Cut out and discard (or reserve for another use) center of bread using a cookie cutter. Heat a small skillet to medium heat. Spread margarine on both sides of bread and place in pan. Break egg into cutout in middle of bread. Cook on one side until egg is partially done and bread is browned. Carefully flip over and cook on other side until done. Transfer to a plate and serve.

1 slice whole-wheat bread
2 teaspoons margarine
1 egg

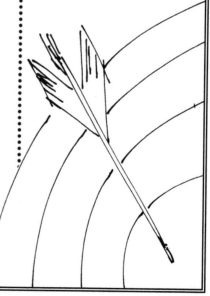

Sweetheart Pancakes

1 3-ounce package
   any red flavor
   sugar-free Jell-O
1½ cups prepared
   pancake batter
½ cup mashed
   banana
Vegetable oil spray

To turn these puffy pink pancakes into heart shapes, either make pancakes in rounds and cut with a heart-shaped cookie cutter or swirl the batter from your spoon into a heart shape right into the pan.

MAKES 1 DOZEN

Add gelatin to prepared pancake batter in a bowl. Mix together well. Stir in banana puree. Cook pancakes in a skillet lightly sprayed with vegetable oil spray over medium-high heat for a few minutes on each side, until lightly browned (but still pink). Serve to your loved ones on Valentine's Day, a special birthday, or any day.

Pancake Puff

This giant popover will give the kids a big thrill.

SERVES 6

Heat oven to 425°F. Beat eggs, flour, and milk together in a bowl until blended. Pour over the melted margarine in a 10-inch round dish sprayed with vegetable oil spray; sprinkle with turkey or ham cubes and cheese. Bake for 25 minutes or until puffy and golden brown. Cut into wedges to serve.

4 eggs
1 cup flour
1 cup skim milk
2 tablespoons margarine, melted
Vegetable oil spray
1 8-ounce slice smoked cooked turkey or ham, cut into ½-inch cubes (about 2 cups)
2 ounces Monterey Jack cheese, cut into ½-inch cubes (about ½ cup)

Corn Cakes

1½ cups stone-
   ground cornmeal
2 tablespoons whole-
   wheat flour
½ teaspoon baking
   soda
¼ teaspoon salt
2 eggs, separated
1½ cups buttermilk
3 tablespoons
   margarine, melted
Vegetable oil spray

Grill up a stack of these corn cakes for a change of pace from plain old pancakes.

MAKES 16

Combine cornmeal, flour, baking soda, and salt in a bowl. In another bowl, beat egg yolks with buttermilk and margarine. Stir into dry ingredients and mix well. Beat egg whites until stiff and fold into batter. Spoon onto a hot griddle sprayed with vegetable oil spray. Cook until browned on both sides. Serve with maple or berry syrup, fruit puree, or jam.

Giant Peach Pancake

Perfect for a special birthday breakfast.
Serve with fresh juice and a side of bacon.

SERVES 4

Heat oven to 450°F. Place margarine in a
10-inch round pan and melt in oven. Beat
eggs and milk together in a bowl. Add flour
and beat until smooth. Pour batter into
pan. Bake for 15 minutes, then reduce heat
to 350°F and bake about 7 minutes longer,
until puffy and golden brown. While baking,
peel and slice peaches and soak in orange
juice to coat. When pancake is done, cover
with sliced peaches and juice. Serve with
cream or sour cream.

1 tablespoon
   margarine
2 eggs
1 cup skim milk
1 cup flour
4 ripe peaches
¼ cup orange juice
¼ cup cream or sour
   cream

Footprints

1 cup whole-wheat
flour
1 cup white flour
1 tablespoon baking
powder
½ teaspoon salt
1 tablespoon light
brown sugar
¼ cup margarine,
melted
1 beaten egg
1¼ cups skim milk
¼ cup finely chopped
pecans
Vegetable oil spray

Watch the kids get their fingerprints all over these yummy Footprints.

MAKES 10

Combine flours, baking powder, salt, and sugar in a bowl. Add margarine, egg, and milk and stir with a fork until moistened. Stir in pecans. Drop batter in peanut shapes onto a hot griddle sprayed with vegetable oil spray. Carefully drop five small dots of batter at one end to make toes (use a turkey baster if desired). Cook until golden brown on both sides. Serve with maple or berry syrup, fruit puree, or jam.

Wonder Waffles

The family will wonder what makes these waffles so good. You don't have to tell them they're full of protein.

MAKES 6

Combine all ingredients in a bowl and beat well. Pour into a heated greased waffle iron and cook until golden brown. Top with melted cheese, margarine, applesauce, or light syrup.

- 2 eggs
- ¼ cup vegetable oil
- 1½ cups skim milk
- 1 cup white flour
- 1 cup whole-wheat flour
- ½ cup shredded cheddar cheese
- 2 teaspoons baking powder
- ¼ teaspoon salt

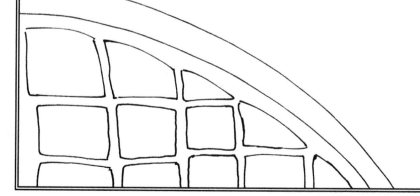

Hole-in-One

Vegetable oil spray
1 8-ounce package
   medium egg
   noodles, cooked
3 eggs, beaten
1 12-ounce can
   evaporated milk
½ cup water
1 6-ounce can water-
   packed tuna,
   drained and flaked
½ pound cheddar
   cheese, shredded
   (about 2 cups)
1 10-ounce package
   frozen peas and
   carrots, thawed

Here's a quick and easy way to serve a complete and healthy breakfast all in one.

SERVES 6

Heat oven to 400°F. Spray a 6-cup muffin tin with vegetable oil spray. Mix all ingredients together. Spoon evenly into muffin cups. Bake for 30–35 minutes. Let cool for 5 to 10 minutes before serving, then loosen edges with a knife and scoop out onto plates. (Freeze and reheat the leftovers.)

Magic Cloud

Full of air, light as a cloud, this magical mixture will have the kids mesmerized.

SERVES 4–6

Heat oven to 400°F. Melt margarine in a saucepan over low heat and blend in flour. Add 2 cups of the milk and cook over medium heat, stirring constantly until thick and bubbly. Pour 1 cup of the mixture into a bowl and stir in slightly beaten egg yolks. Beat egg whites until stiff but not dry. Gently fold yolk mixture into egg whites. Turn into an ungreased 8-inch round baking dish. Bake for 15 minutes, until puffy and golden brown. Meanwhile, stir cheese into remaining milk mixture and heat and stir until melted. Add remaining 1/3 cup milk, remove from heat, and serve over Magic Cloud.

1/4 cup margarine
1/3 cup flour
2 1/3 cups skim milk
4 eggs, separated
1 cup shredded
   cheddar cheese

Super Hero-to-Go

4 eggs
³⁄₈ cup skim milk
2 6-inch-long hero
   rolls, cut in half
   lengthwise
2 tablespoons
   margarine
Vegetable oil spray
¼ cup crumbled
   cooked bacon
¼ cup shredded
   cheddar cheese

A hearty high-protein breakfast the kids can eat on their run for the school bus.

MAKES 2

Beat eggs and milk together. Spread bottom of each roll with margarine and toast under broiler until golden. Spray a skillet with vegetable oil spray and place over medium heat. Add egg and milk mixture along with crumbled bacon. Cook and stir until eggs are set. Spoon egg mixture onto 2 roll halves, sprinkle with cheddar cheese, and top with remaining roll halves.

Dinosaur Eggs

Serve the amateur archaeologists these giant Dinosaur Eggs to keep them going on their eggciting expeditions.

MAKES 4

Heat oven to 350°F. Spread margarine on both sides of bread slices and place each in a 6-ounce custard cup; press in gently. Beat eggs, milk, and cheese together in a bowl. Pour into bread cups. Bake for 15 minutes or until egg is set.

2 tablespoons margarine
4 slices whole-wheat bread
4 eggs
¼ cup skim milk
½ cup grated Swiss cheese

Muggies

½ teaspoon
   margarine
2 eggs
2 teaspoons skim
   milk
¼ cup shredded
   cheddar cheese

What fun these mugs full of eggs are for the kids—and so easy to make!

MAKES 1

Put margarine in a microwave-safe mug. Microwave on high for 20–30 seconds to melt margarine. Break eggs into mug. Add milk and mix with fork. Microwave on high for 1 minute. Stir with a fork to break apart and microwave for 20 seconds more. Remove while still soft and moist but cooked. Sprinkle cheese on top and serve in mug.

Sweetheart Eggs

A quick, easy, and fun way to say "I love you" in the morning.

1 teaspoon margarine
Heart-shaped metal
   cookie cutter
1 egg

MAKES 1

Melt margarine in a small saucepan. Place cookie cutter in center of pan. Break egg into cookie cutter and press cutter into pan for a few seconds (wear a mitt to avoid burning yourself). Cook egg sunny-side up until done, then serve heart-shaped egg to loved one.

Ham and Egg Sandwich

1 6-ounce can chunk-style ham
2 tablespoons fine dry bread crumbs
6 tablespoons skim milk
4 eggs, 1 separated
2 tablespoons margarine
Vegetable oil spray

This fancy breakfast will delight your kids on special days. It's much more fun to eat than ordinary bread, ham, and egg.

MAKES 2

Preheat oven to 350°F. Flake ham into a bowl. Stir in bread crumbs, 2 tablespoons of the milk, and the egg white. In another bowl, stir together remaining eggs and egg yolk and remaining milk. Heat margarine in a skillet until melted. Stir in egg-milk mixture and cook until partially set. Remove from heat. Spray two 1-cup casserole dishes with vegetable oil spray. Place ¼ cup ham mixture in each dish and spread evenly over bottom. Top each with half of the scrambled egg mixture. Add remaining ham mixture and press down lightly. Bake for 15–20 minutes until heated through. Carefully unmold onto serving plate.

Create a fun-to-eat atmosphere. A stressful dining table can create eating disorders and can discourage kids from trying new foods. Instead of talking about problems or giving lectures, how about playing games, discussing the best part of your day, playing music, listening to books on tape, or asking the kids to rate the food. Give them a chart so they can grade the meal in different categories, such as name, taste, texture, color, and so on. Give the kids plenty of time to eat so they don't feel rushed.

Breakfast Cookies

Vegetable oil spray
½ cup (1 stick)
    margarine,
    softened
⅓ cup honey
1 egg
⅓ cup whole-bran
    cereal
¼ cup orange juice
1½ teaspoons vanilla
    extract

Cookies for breakfast? You bet—when they're made the nutritious way.

MAKES 3 DOZEN

Heat oven to 350°F. Spray one or two cookie sheets with vegetable oil spray. Cream together margarine and honey in a large bowl. Beat in egg. Add bran, juice, and vanilla and mix well. Add flour, baking powder, baking soda, salt, dry milk, and oatmeal. Mix well. Stir in nuts and raisins. Drop tablespoonfuls 2 inches apart onto cookie sheets. Bake for 10–12 minutes, until golden brown.

To store: These may be refrigerated in an airtight container for up to 1 week or frozen for up to 2 months.

Do something crazy with the food every now and then. Serve everyone breakfast in bed when it's not a special occasion. Tint the meal all different colors with food coloring or make it all one color on special holidays. For example, on St. Patrick's Day, serve green salad, green pizza dough with green bell pepper slices, and green milk shakes. Or have a picnic in the family room on a large blanket. Or serve the meal backward one day—dessert first, then main course, then salad. Or serve the food in strange ways, such as in Chinese take-out boxes or on bandanna place mats.

1 cup flour
1 teaspoon baking powder
1/2 teaspoon baking soda
1/4 teaspoon salt
1/3 cup nonfat dry milk
1 cup rolled oats
1 cup chopped nuts
1 cup raisins

Circus Crunch

1/4 cup margarine, melted
1 tablespoon Worcestershire sauce
1/2 cup crispy corn Chex cereal
1/2 cup crispy wheat Chex cereal
1/2 cup unsalted roasted peanuts, chopped
1/4 cup raisins
1/8 teaspoon garlic or onion powder

Who says you have to have soggy cereal for breakfast? Why not keep it crunchy and pretend you're having breakfast at the circus?

SERVES 2–4

Heat oven to 325°F. Mix margarine with Worcestershire sauce and set aside. In a large bowl, combine remaining ingredients. Drizzle margarine mixture over cereal and toss well. Spread on a large baking sheet and bake, stirring occasionally, until lightly toasted, about 25–30 minutes.

To store: These may be refrigerated in an airtight container for up to 2 weeks or frozen for up to 3 months.

Zoo Food

Here's a new way to serve boring old oatmeal. Jazz it up with a little heat, a few nuts, and some fruit.

MAKES 4 CUPS

Heat oven to 400°F. Combine oats, nuts, and wheat germ. Spread in a 15" × 10" × 1" baking pan. Toast in oven for 10 minutes, stirring occasionally. Remove from heat and stir in raisins, apricots, and brown sugar if desired. Pour into bowls and serve with milk.

To store: This may be refrigerated in an airtight container for up to 2 weeks or frozen for up to 3 months.

1½ cups quick-cooking oats
½ cup chopped peanuts
½ cup chopped almonds
½ cup wheat germ
½ cup raisins
⅓ cup chopped dried apricots
¼ cup packed light brown sugar (optional)
Skim milk

Branana Balls

Vegetable oil spray
2 cups wheat bran cereal (not flakes)
½ cup skim milk
2 bananas, mashed (1 cup)
⅓ cup margarine
¼ cup sugar
1 teaspoon vanilla extract
1 egg
1 cup flour
2 teaspoons baking powder
½ teaspoon salt
½ cup raisins

Combine potassium-loaded bananas with high-fiber bran cereal and you've got a great power breakfast for the kids.

MAKES 1 DOZEN

Heat oven to 400°F. Spray a 12-cup muffin tin with vegetable oil spray. Combine cereal, milk, and bananas and mix well. Cream together margarine, sugar, and vanilla in a large bowl. Beat in egg. Beat in banana-bran mixture. Combine flour, baking powder, and salt; add to mixture. Stir until just blended. Add raisins. Spoon into muffin cups and bake for 18–20 minutes, until lightly browned.

To store: These may be refrigerated in an airtight container for up to 1 week or frozen for up to 2 months.

Potato Chippers

These are like giant tasty potato chips, but Potato Chippers are good for you and make a great breakfast.

MAKES 1 DOZEN

Spray a griddle or skillet with vegetable oil spray. Combine all ingredients and spoon onto hot griddle; flatten each cake with a spatula. Cook over medium heat 5–7 minutes, flipping once, until both sides are browned. Drain on paper towel and serve with jelly, nonfat sour cream, nonfat cottage cheese, or margarine.

Vegetable oil spray
2 eggs
1 small onion, chopped
2 tablespoons flour
1/4 teaspoon baking powder
1/4 teaspoon salt
3 cups shredded raw potatoes

Sunrise Surprise Muffins

8 oranges

1 egg

3/4 cup skim milk

1 tablespoon
   margarine, melted

1/2 cup cornmeal

1/2 cup whole-wheat
   flour

1/2 cup white flour

1 teaspoon baking
   powder

1/2 teaspoon salt

1 16-ounce can corn,
   drained

Wake up your sleepyheads with these eye-opening muffins. They're a meal in one and so much fun to peel and eat.

MAKES 8

Heat oven to 400°F. Slice tops off oranges and remove pulp and juice. (Strain juice and save to serve with muffins.) In a bowl, beat egg slightly. Mix in milk and margarine. Add cornmeal, flours, baking powder, and salt and blend. Stir in corn and spoon mixture into hollowed-out orange shells. Set shells in a muffin tin and bake for 20–25 minutes. Peel and eat.

To store: These may be refrigerated in an airtight container for up to 1 week or frozen for up to 2 months.

5
Lightning Lunches

Funny Face Sandwich

A funny face to greet the kids at lunchtime.

MAKES 8

Heat oven to 400°F. Combine mayonnaise, onion, and cheese in a bowl. Separate dough into eight biscuits. Roll each into a 4-inch circle on an ungreased cookie sheet. Place a tomato slice on each biscuit. Spread mayonnaise mixture on top of tomato. Make a face using bacon bits— eyes, nose, mouth, hair. Bake for 10–12 minutes, until golden brown. Cool for a few minutes before serving.

Variation: To add to your funny face, use pimiento pieces, olives, raisins, seeds, vegetable cutouts, and other additions.

¼ cup mayonnaise
¼ cup chopped onion
¼ cup shredded
   Swiss cheese
1 8-ounce can flaky
   refrigerator
   biscuits
   (8 biscuits)
8 thin slices tomato
8 slices bacon,
   cooked, drained,
   and crumbled

Jack and Jill Lunch

1 slice whole-wheat
  bread, toasted
1 hard-cooked egg,
  peeled and cut in
  half lengthwise
¼ cup grated
  cheddar or
  Monterey Jack
  cheese
Raisins, Cheerios, or
  other cereal
1 carrot or celery
  stick, cut into 8
  strips

We call them Jack and Jill, but you can name them after your own kids or some special cartoon friends. Set out the ingredients and let the kids create their own Jack and Jill Lunch.

SERVES 1

Cut toast in half diagonally to form two triangles. Place one triangle pointing down for Jack and one pointing up for Jill. Place hard-cooked egg at top of both for heads and top heads with grated cheese for hair. Add raisins or cereal for eyes, nose, mouth, and buttons down the front of the triangles. (A small slice of celery cut crosswise makes a nice smile.) Add carrot or celery sticks for arms and legs.

Animal Farm

These triple-decker sandwiches are fun to play with, so let the kids have a good time before they gobble them up.

MAKES 2 CUTOUT SANDWICHES

Cut out two animal shapes from each slice of bread using two different cookie cutters. (Use the same shape three times to make three of each animal.) Spread tuna or jam on one animal cutout. Top with another animal cutout and spread with peanut butter or cream cheese. Top with another animal cutout. Now stand the animal up on the plate and let the kids play with and eat their Animal Farm.

1 6-ounce can water-packed tuna, drained, flaked, and mixed with 2 tablespoons mayonnaise, or 2 tablespoons fruit jam
3 slices bread
Animal cookie cutters
¼ cup creamy peanut butter or cream cheese

Turkey Gobblers

2 slices raisin bread,
   toasted
1 tablespoon
   margarine
¼ cup whole
   cranberry sauce
2 slices cooked
   turkey
2 slices Swiss cheese
2 slices pineapple,
   well drained

A great way to serve Thanksgiving leftovers or celebrate Turkey Day the rest of the year.

MAKES 2

Heat the broiler. Spread margarine on one side of each slice of toast. Then spread with cranberry sauce. Top each with a slice of turkey, then cheese, then pineapple. Broil for 3–4 minutes, until cheese is melted.

Under-the-Seawich

Tuna offers lots of ways to jazz up the noontime sandwich. Try this recipe or some of the variations.

MAKES 2

Mix tuna, pineapple, water chestnuts if desired, and mayonnaise together and spread on two slices bread. Top with remaining slices.

Variations:
- Tuna plus 2 tablespoons minced celery, 2 teaspoons sweet pickle relish, and 2 tablespoons mayonnaise
- Tuna plus 2 hard-cooked eggs and 3 tablespoons mayonnaise or salad dressing
- Tuna plus 2 tablespoons minced cucumber, 1 tablespoon minced green bell pepper, and 2 tablespoons mayonnaise

1 6-ounce can water-packed tuna, drained and flaked

½ cup drained crushed pineapple

⅓ cup chopped drained water chestnuts (optional)

2 tablespoons mayonnaise

4 slices whole-wheat bread

Kaleidoscopes

½ cup cream cheese
  or peanut butter
  (creamy or chunky)
4 slices bread,
  crusts removed
8 thin slices salami
  or 4 slices ham or
  bologna
4 slices cheese
Toothpicks (optional)

Sometimes just the shape of a sandwich can make all the difference.

MAKES 4

Spread cream cheese or peanut butter on bread. Layer on two slices of salami or one slice of ham or bologna. Add one slice of cheese. Roll up into a kaleidoscope, secure with a toothpick if needed, and serve.

Little Devil Sandwiches

Add a little pizzazz to deviled ham to make this lunch a tasty treat for the kids.

MAKES 1

Mix ham with pineapple and bell pepper. Spread on a slice of raisin bread. Top with remaining slice of bread.

Variations:
- Ham with 1 tablespoon minced celery and 1 teaspoon yellow mustard
- Ham with 1 hard-cooked egg, peeled and chopped, 2 teaspoons sweet pickle relish, and 1 tablespoon mayonnaise
- Ham with 2 tablespoons shredded Swiss cheese and 1 tablespoon mayonnaise
- Ham with 2 tablespoons chopped apple and 1 tablespoon mayonnaise

1 2-ounce can deviled ham
1 tablespoon crushed pineapple
1 tablespoon minced green bell pepper
2 slices raisin bread

Sticky Stuff Sandwiches

2 slices whole-wheat
  bread
1 tablespoon peanut
  butter

PLUS:
1 tablespoon finely
  chopped celery OR
1 tablespoon chopped
  raisins OR
½ banana, peeled and
  mashed OR
2 tablespoons
  chopped apple OR
1 teaspoon sweet
  pickle relish OR
½ tablespoon honey
  OR
2 slices salami or
  1 slice bologna or
  ham

Peanut butter, the kids' favorite taste, has tremendous versatility. Try some of these peanut butter combinations for a change.

MAKES 1

Lightly toast bread, if desired. Mix together peanut butter and other ingredients. Spread on one slice of bread and top with the other.

Yo-Yos

A new way to serve an old favorite. Choose low-fat turkey franks if you prefer.

MAKES 6

Heat the broiler. Top each baguette slice with one turkey frank round. Sprinkle on cheddar cheese and dot with an olive half in the middle. Broil for 5–7 minutes, until cheese has melted.

6 round slices
   baguette
1 turkey frank, sliced
   into 6 rounds
¼ cup grated
   cheddar cheese
3 pitted black olives,
   sliced in half

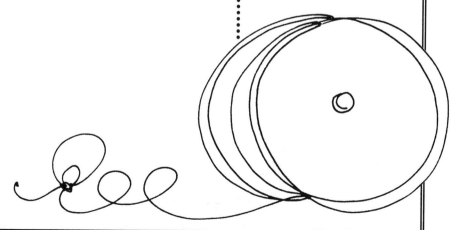

Henny-Penny Sandwiches

2 slices whole-wheat
   bread
1 hard-cooked egg,
   peeled and chopped

PLUS:
2 salami slices or
   1 bologna slice or
   ham slice, chopped,
   and ½ tablespoon
   mayonnaise OR

1 teaspoon chopped
   pitted black olives,
   1 teaspoon
   chopped celery,
   1 teaspoon
   chopped carrot,
   and ½ tablespoon
   mayonnaise OR

When she's not worrying about the sky
falling, Henny-Penny is whipping up these
yummy egg sandwich variations.

MAKES 1

Lightly toast bread, if desired. Mix
together egg and other ingredients.
Spread on one slice of bread and top
with the other. Try a new combination each
day.

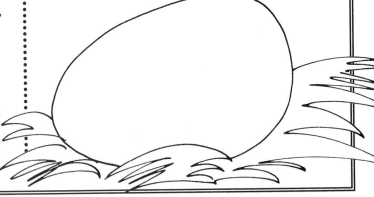

Make the lunchbox more fun. Add notes, comics cut from the morning paper, or little surprises like stickers, pencils, cute paper napkins, or plastic toys. Vary the lunch each day so it's not the same old thing. Make a week's worth of sandwiches at a time to help you with packing on those rushed mornings. Wrap the foods well so they're still appealing hours later. Include you-put-it-together lunches to keep foods fresh and give the kids a chance to create their own lunches. Vary the thermos filling too—chocolate milk, apple juice, hot cider, hot soup.

1 teaspoon chopped bell pepper, ½ teaspoon sweet pickle relish, and ½ tablespoon mayonnaise OR

1 slice bacon, cooked, drained, and crumbled, and ½ tablespoon mayonnaise OR

2 teaspoons shredded Swiss cheese and ½ tablespoon mayonnaise

Stars and Planets

1 ½-pound block
 cheddar cheese
1 ½-pound block
 Monterey Jack
 cheese
1 ½-inch-thick slice
 ham, salami, or
 bologna
1 small rectangular
 sourdough
 sandwich roll,
 sliced about ½
 inch thick

A lunch that's out of this world, yet so easy to create and so much fun to eat.

SERVES 2

Slice cheese into ½-inch-thick slabs. Cut out shapes using star and circle cookie cutters, large or small. Cut out meat with cookie cutters. Slice crust off bread. Cut out bread with cookie cutters. Place all stars and planets in plastic container or large plastic bag to place in lunchbox or serve on a plate. Let the kids put them together or eat each item separately. Serve with small packets of ketchup, mustard, or mayonnaise for dipping.

Heart of Gold Muffins

Don't tell the kids what's inside. Finding out for themselves is half the fun.

MAKES 8

Heat oven to 400°F. Prepare corn bread/muffin mix according to package directions. Generously spray an 8-cup muffin tin with vegetable oil spray and fill muffin cups with batter. Cut turkey franks into quarters and push into center of muffin batter. Cover franks with batter and bake according to package directions. When done, remove from oven and stick ice cream sticks through center of muffins. Serve to kids with ketchup and mustard.

1 8-ounce package corn bread/muffin mix
Vegetable oil spray
2 turkey franks
8 ice cream sticks
Ketchup and mustard

Puff Pillows

2 turkey franks
20 wonton wrappers
1 beef bouillon cube
Ketchup and mustard

Let the kids make these bite-size Puff Pillows with you.

MAKES 10

Cut each frank into five pieces. Place one piece on a wonton wrapper and top with another wrapper. Pinch the edges closed, using a little water to make them stick. Boil in water with a beef bouillon cube for 2–3 minutes. Drain on a paper towel and serve with ketchup and mustard.

Pizza Pinwheels

They look like pinwheels, but they taste like pizza.

MAKES 16

Heat oven to 350°F. Separate dough into four rectangles. Press perforation together to seal. Brush rectangles with pizza sauce. Place 8 salami slices on each rectangle. Sprinkle with cheese. Tightly roll up dough from a short side and pinch to seal. Slice each roll into four equal slices. Pinch dough together on one cut side of each slice to seal. Place on an ungreased cookie sheet sealed side down and bake for 20 minutes, until golden brown.

1 8-ounce package
   refrigerator
   crescent rolls
   (8 rolls)
1 cup pizza sauce
32 thin slices salami
½ cup shredded
   mozzarella cheese

Pizza Cake

2 tablespoons pizza
   sauce
1 rice cake
2 tablespoons grated
   mozzarella,
   cheddar, or
   Monterey Jack
   cheese

This quick and easy lunch is a piece of cake. Make that a Pizza Cake. Add toppings if you like or leave it plain. For more variety, substitute an English muffin, a bagel, or a warmed tortilla for the rice cake.

MAKES 1

Heat oven to 350°F. Spoon sauce over rice cake. Sprinkle on cheese. Add any toppings you wish. Bake for 8–10 minutes or heat in microwave for 1–2 minutes, until cheese is bubbly.

Wolfman Wieners

Even the young and pure at heart may howl likes wolves when they open their mouths and eat these wiener bites.

MAKES 4 DOZEN

Heat oven to 375°F. Separate dough into 16 triangles. Cut each triangle lengthwise into thirds. Place sausage on shortest side of each triangle. Roll up, starting at shortest side and rolling to opposite point. Place on an ungreased cookie sheet. Bake for 12–15 minutes, until golden brown. Serve with ketchup and mustard.

2 8-ounce cans refrigerator crescent rolls (16 rolls total)
48 fully cooked small turkey sausage links
Ketchup and mustard

Cottontails

1 8-ounce package
   refrigerator
   crescent rolls
   (8 rolls)

PLUS:
½ cup peanut butter
¼ cup jelly OR
4 slices ham
4 slices cheese

Vegetable oil spray

Use your imagination and fill these Cottontails with different sandwich surprises. Here are two suggestions.

MAKES 4

Heat oven to 400°F. Unroll dough, leaving triangles attached to form four rectangles. Use a fork to seal the perforation. Roll or stretch dough until it is the size of two slices of bread. Repeat with rest of dough. Put sandwich filling on one half, leaving ½ inch uncovered on all sides. Fold over and seal edges with fork. Then round the edges to form circles. Cook according to package directions on a cookie sheet sprayed with vegetable oil spray. Eat right from the oven (after allowing to cool a little) or pack in lunchboxes to be eaten cold.

Boulder Bites

Anytime you can present a fun food in a new package, you'll get a look of delight from your child. Make a bunch of these Boulder Bites and freeze them until you need them.

MAKES 4

Heat oven to 375°F. Unroll dough and separate into four rectangles. Pinch perforations to seal. Stir chicken, cheese, apricots, and softened cream cheese together in a bowl. Divide among rectangles of dough, mounding in the center of each rectangle. Bring corners of dough over filling and pinch closed to seal. Bake on ungreased cookie sheet for 15 minutes, until golden brown. Cool and serve or freeze, then pack in lunchboxes to thaw by lunchtime.

1 8-ounce package refrigerator crescent rolls (8 rolls)

2 5-ounce cans chunk-style chicken or turkey, drained and flaked

1/2 cup shredded cheddar cheese

1/4 cup chopped dried apricots

1 3-ounce package cream cheese, softened

Pockets Full of Fun

1 6½-ounce can
    water-packed tuna,
    drained
1 carrot, shredded
½ 6-inch zucchini,
    shredded
1 apple, cored and
    finely chopped
4 teaspoons
    mayonnaise
1 teaspoon poppy
    seeds or wheat
    germ (optional)
2 whole-wheat pita
    breads

Kids love to find things in their pockets. Fill these pockets with fun—and good nutrition.

MAKES 4

Combine tuna, carrot, zucchini, and apple with mayonnaise and poppy seeds if desired. Cut breads in half and fill pockets with tuna mixture.

Teddy Bear Tails

This peanut butter sandwich made with muffins makes a unique lunch that's packed with protein and fiber.

2 bran muffins
¼ cup peanut butter
   (creamy or chunky)
2 tablespoons raisins

MAKES 2

Cut muffins in half and hollow out centers. Fill with peanut butter mixed with raisins. Seal closed with peanut butter.

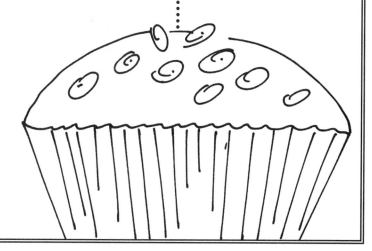

Bagel Islands

4 plain, onion, or
   garlic minibagels
¼ cup cream cheese
2 apples, cored and
   sliced into eighths
2 celery ribs from the
   heart with leaves,
   sliced thin
   lengthwise into
   fourths

Shipwreck the kids on Bagel Island—they'll
have to eat their way back home!

MAKES 8

Slice bagels in half. Spread cream cheese
on each half. Place two apple slices on each
half, facing each other. Place celery "trees"
in center of island.

**To lower salt: Don't add salt to
foods. Let the natural taste delight
the kids. Leave the saltshaker off
the table. Use unsalted products
from the store. Make homemade
foods using less or no salt. Read
labels.**

Burger Wieners

Who says hamburgers can't be hot dogs? Here's a fun way to serve an old favorite that's also pumped up with more good nutrition.

MAKES 6

Heat the broiler. Combine cereal, sour cream, egg, and onion in a bowl. Add ground beef and mix well. Shape into six logs to fit buns. Broil for 10 minutes, until done, turning occasionally. Serve in hot dog buns with condiments.

¼ cup finely crushed oat flakes or other cereal
¼ cup low-fat sour cream
1 egg, slightly beaten
½ teaspoon dry minced onion
1 pound lean ground beef
6 hot dog buns, toasted

Chili-Chick

2 sourdough rolls,
   unsliced
1 8-ounce can chili
1 6-ounce can chunk-
   style chicken,
   drained and flaked

A hot, hefty sandwich to reheat the body and warm the spirit.

MAKES 2

Using a sharp knife, cut into bread on one end and hollow out insides without cutting completely through bread. Heat chili and chicken together in a saucepan. Spoon into opening at one end of bread roll until filled. Stick a piece of bread from the inside in the cut end to close and serve.

Variation: Cut the top off a small round individual sourdough loaf and hollow out insides. Fill with chili-chicken mixture, beef stew, corned beef hash, or other thick hot mixture. Recover with bread top and serve. Kids can eat the whole thing—stew inside and bread bowl container.

Quackers

Peanut butter crackers are fun to eat for lunch instead of everyday sandwiches. And these have a surprise inside!

MAKES 8

Spread peanut butter in a circular motion on eight crackers, leaving center of crackers uncovered. Fill empty center with jelly. Top with remaining crackers and serve.

Variation: Fill crackers with round slices of cheese and thinly sliced apple circles.

½ cup peanut butter (creamy or chunky)
16 whole-wheat crackers
¼ cup jelly

Shrunken Sandwiches

12 Ritz Bits peanut
butter sandwich
crackers
2 slices cooked ham
2 slices American
cheese

Honey, we've shrunk the sandwiches—and boy, are they fun to eat!

MAKES 1 DOZEN

Open sandwich crackers. Cut ham and cheese into small rounds (6 from each slice) the size of the Ritz Bits crackers (use a clean medicine bottle as a cutter to make it easy). Put ham on peanut butter part of cracker, then cheese. Cover with the other half of the cracker.

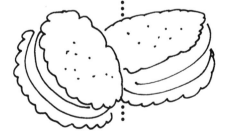

Phony Baloney

No baloney about it—these skewered treats are a delight to eat.

MAKES 2

Heat the broiler. Thread skewers alternately with pineapple chunks, pepper squares, and bologna squares. Broil for 5–7 minutes, turning often, until sizzling. Serve on hot dog buns with ketchup and mustard mixed together.

2 skewers
1 4-ounce can pineapple chunks, drained
1 green bell pepper, cut into 1-inch squares
4 slices bologna, cut into 1-inch squares
2 hot dog buns, toasted
Ketchup and mustard

Red Balloons

1 10-ounce package
    frozen green peas
    with carrots or
    corn
¼ teaspoon dried dill
2 teaspoons green
    goddess, ranch, or
    thousand island
    salad dressing
4 large ripe tomatoes

A colorful and unique way to package lunch for the kids and get them to eat their vegetables. Red Balloons also go great as a side dish with dinner.

MAKES 4

Cook frozen vegetables according to package directions. Mix together dill and salad dressing and stir into vegetables. Cut tops off tomatoes and hollow out centers. Fill tomatoes with vegetable mixture. Refrigerate for 1 hour before serving.

Variation: Stuff with pasta salad, tuna salad, egg salad, chicken salad, or potato salad.

Jungle Swamp

This chili fondue makes a great lunch to warm the tummies on cold days.

SERVES 2

Combine chili with cheese in a saucepan and heat over medium heat until cheese is melted. Blend water with cornstarch and add to chili-cheese mixture. Cook and stir until bubbly. Pour into a bowl and serve in center of table with cut-up turkey franks and French bread cubes for dunking on skewers.

1 10-ounce can chili
½ cup shredded cheddar cheese
⅓ cup cold water
1 tablespoon cornstarch
2 turkey franks, cut up
French bread, cut into bite-size cubes
2 skewers or fondue forks

Shark Bait Soup

2½ cups milk
1 10-ounce can cream
   of mushroom soup
1 10-ounce can cream
   of chicken soup
1 7-ounce can water-
   packed tuna,
   drained and flaked

A hearty seafood soup for tuna lovers.

SERVES 4

Pour milk into a saucepan with soups. Stir until blended. Add flaked tuna and simmer over medium heat for 10 minutes.

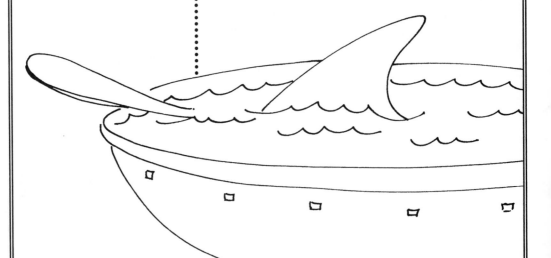

Sandwich Puzzles

They look like cookies, they go together like a puzzle, but they taste like sandwiches! Give the kids a sandwich bag full of fun-to-eat and fun-to-play-with Sandwich Puzzles.

MAKES 3

Combine tuna, egg, relish, mayonnaise, and mustard in a bowl and mix well. Divide mixture among three slices of bread. Place a second slice of bread on top of each. Press out shapes using cookie cutters. Cut remaining pieces of sandwich into creative shapes. Slip a note in with the sandwich that says "See if you can put this sandwich puzzle together!"

1 6-ounce can water-packed tuna, drained
1 hard-cooked egg, peeled and chopped
2 teaspoons sweet pickle relish
3 tablespoons mayonnaise
1 teaspoon yellow mustard
6 slices soft whole-wheat bread

6
Dynamite Dinners

Dinosaur Bites

These may be big servings to the kids, but they're just tiny little bites to a great big dinosaur. Be creative with your servings and your stuffings.

MAKES 8

Heat oven to 350°F. Spray an 8-cup muffin tin with vegetable oil spray. Mix everything except sesame seeds together. Divide among muffin cups. Top with sesame seeds and bake for 20 minutes.

Variations: Add any of these:
- ¼ cup chopped nuts
- ½ cup grated cheese
- ½ cup shredded apple or chopped apricots
- ½ cup shredded zucchini, shredded carrot, or peas

Vegetable oil spray
1 pound lean ground meat
¼ cup wheat germ
2 tablespoons minced onion
1 egg, beaten
¼ cup skim milk
¼ cup tomato sauce
Sesame seeds

Ham-I-Am

½ cup shredded
    carrot
¼ cup chopped onion
2 tablespoons
    margarine
3 tablespoons flour
1 quart skim milk
1½ cups diced cooked
    ham
1 celery rib, finely
    chopped
½ teaspoon
    Worcestershire
    sauce
1 cup cubed American
    cheese

That Sam-I-Am loves Ham-I-Am, and so will your kids. It's a great way to pack a whole meal into one dish.

SERVES 4–6

Cook carrot and onion in margarine in a large saucepan over medium heat until tender. Blend in flour. Add milk. Cook and stir until thickened and bubbly. Stir in diced ham, celery, and Worcestershire and heat through. Add cheese and stir until melted. Serve in bowls or on plates.

Puff Muffins

A puffy crown over an English muffin makes a special surprise dinner.

SERVES 4

Heat oven to 375°F. Toast muffin or bun halves. Spread each half with deviled ham, then with corn. Beat egg yolks and mustard until thick and lemon colored. Fold in shredded cheese. Beat whites until stiff but not dry. Fold whites into yolk mixture. Spoon onto muffins, spreading just to the edges. Bake on an ungreased cookie sheet for 12–15 minutes, until golden.

4 English muffins or hamburger buns, split
1 4-ounce can deviled ham
1 8-ounce can corn, drained
3 eggs, separated
1/2 teaspoon yellow mustard
1/2 cup shredded American cheese

Invisible Dinner

½ pound lean ground beef

¼ cup chopped onion

1 8-ounce can pizza sauce

2 tablespoons chopped pitted black olives

1 teaspoon dried basil, crushed

½ teaspoon dried oregano, crushed

3 individual French rolls, about 8 inches long

1½ cups shredded mozzarella cheese

Set this seemingly ordinary roll on the kids' plates and tell them that's dinner—the rest is invisible.

MAKES 3

Heat oven to 375°F. Cook meat and onion in a skillet over medium heat until meat is brown; drain. Stir in pizza sauce, olives, and seasonings. Cut roll in half lengthwise and hollow out insides to within ½ inch of edges. Sprinkle half the cheese into bottom of each roll. Spoon meat mixture over cheese. Sprinkle in remaining cheese. Replace roll tops. Wrap in foil and bake for 20 minutes.

Swamp Thing

Who knows what lurks inside this mysterious Swamp Thing?

MAKES 6

Heat oven to 425°F. Melt margarine in a saucepan. Add corn bread stuffing mix. Combine egg and water; add to stuffing mixture and mix well. Press mixture into bottom and up sides of six individual baking dishes. Bake for 10 minutes. Meanwhile, cook vegetables according to package directions. Add cheese, stirring to melt. Add ham and heat through. Spoon ham mixture into baked stuffing shells and serve.

6 tablespoons margarine
3 cups corn bread stuffing mix
1 egg, slightly beaten
1/4 cup water
2 8-ounce packages frozen mixed vegetables
1/2 cup shredded cheddar cheese
2 cups cubed cooked ham

Holiday Ornaments

4 large tomatoes
1½ cups favorite
   meat loaf recipe
4 slices American
   cheese
Cheese spread

Every day's a holiday when you serve these bright ornamental balls. Decorate the outsides using a pastry bag filled with cheese spread.

MAKES 4

Heat the broiler. Cut tops off tomatoes and scoop out pulp. Mix with meat loaf recipe. Bake meat loaf according to your recipe instructions. When done, stuff tomatoes with crumbled meat loaf. Cut cheese slices into fun shapes with a cookie cutter. Lay cheese cutouts on top of meat loaf–filled tomatoes and heat under the broiler for 3–5 minutes, until cheese melts a little. Remove from heat and decorate sides of tomato with cheese spread in a pastry bag.

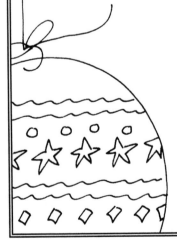

Detective Dinner

Unless they're great detectives, the kids won't have a clue as to what vegetable you've got hidden away in this disguised dinner dish. Feel free to stash away other vegetable evidence in this tasty but puzzling casserole that covers all four food groups.

SERVES 4

Heat oven to 350°F. Cook broccoli according to package directions. Mix together with chicken, mayonnaise, soup, cheese, and onion. Pour into a 3-quart casserole dish, top with crushed crackers, and bake for 30 minutes.

1 10-ounce package frozen broccoli or other vegetable, cooked

1 cup cubed cooked chicken or ham

½ cup mayonnaise

1 10-ounce can cream of chicken soup

1 cup cubed American cheese

1 tablespoon minced onion

¼ cup crushed whole-wheat crackers

Secret Surprise Pie

1⅛ cups flour
1/4 cup vegetable oil
3 tablespoons skim
   milk
4 eggs
1 10-ounce can cream
   of celery or cream
   of mushroom soup
½ cup half-and-half
1 cup shredded
   cheddar cheese
½ cup diced cooked
   chicken
½ cup frozen peas

A meal in one that will serve the whole family and have them asking for more.

SERVES 6–8

Heat oven to 350°F. Pour flour into a bowl, add oil and milk and mix lightly with a fork. Form into a ball, roll out between sheets of wax paper with a rolling pin, remove wax paper, and place dough circle in a 9-inch pie pan. Beat eggs until foamy. Add soup and half-and-half and mix well. Sprinkle cheese, chicken, and peas over piecrust. Pour soup mixture over. Bake for 50 minutes or until center is set. Let stand for 10 minutes before serving.

Variation: Use cubed cooked ham and chopped cooked broccoli instead of chicken and peas.

Peanut Butter Burgers

They may sound strange to you, but the kids think these Peanut Butter Burgers taste just right.

SERVES 4

Combine eggs, beef, onion, and peanut butter and shape into four patties. Broil for 6–8 minutes, turning once. Top with dill pickle slices if desired and serve in toasted hamburger buns with your choice of condiments.

2 eggs, lightly beaten
1 pound lean ground beef
¼ cup chopped onion
¼ cup chunky peanut butter
Dill pickles, sliced (optional)
4 hamburger buns, split and toasted

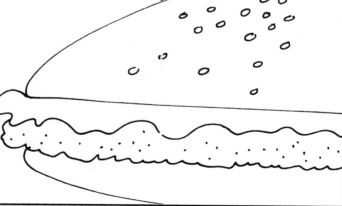

Burger Buddies

1/4 pound sliced
    luncheon meat,
    chopped
1/8 cup chopped
    pitted black olives
1/8 cup chopped celery
1/2 cup shredded
    American cheese
1/8 cup ketchup
1 tablespoon chopped
    onion
4 hamburger buns,
    split and toasted

Great for camping trips or backyard overnighters.

SERVES 4

Heat oven to 400°F. Combine meat with olives and celery. Stir in cheese, ketchup, and onion. Spread on bottom halves of hamburger buns. Top with remaining halves and wrap individually in foil. Bake for 15–20 minutes.

Sloppy Jack-O'-Lanterns

Here's a great way to get them to eat their burgers and sandwiches.

MAKES 4

Cook ground beef and prepare Sloppy Joes according to package directions. Divide mixture among four hamburger buns and place on plates. Cut out triangle eyes and noses and crescent mouths from cheese slices and place on outside of bun to form jack-o'-lantern faces.

1 pound lean ground beef
1 1½-ounce package Sloppy Joe mix
4 hamburger buns
4 cheese slices

Teeny Tiny Tacos

Vegetable oil spray
1 pound lean ground
    beef
1 1½-ounce package
    taco seasoning
¼ cup shredded
    carrot
¼ cup chopped onion
1 8-ounce package
    refrigerator
    biscuits
    (8 biscuits)
½ cup grated
    cheddar cheese
¼ cup chopped
    tomato
Yellow mustard or
    taco sauce

Teeny tiny tacos for teeny tiny mouths—a different way to serve an old favorite.

MAKES 8

Heat oven to 400°F and spray a cookie sheet with vegetable oil spray. Brown ground beef in a skillet and drain. Mix with taco seasoning according to package directions and add carrot and onion. Roll each biscuit into a thin flat round. Divide meat mixture among biscuits, placing it on one half of each round. Add cheese and tomato, fold uncovered side over, and press edges together with a fork or your fingers. Place on cookie sheet and bake according to directions on biscuit package until brown. Serve with mustard or taco sauce.

Mexican Pyramids

The kids will toss these fun-filled Mexican Pyramids right into their tummies.

MAKES 1

Spray a small skillet with vegetable oil spray and place one tortilla in pan. Sprinkle on cheese, bacon, olives, and chilies and cover with second tortilla. Heat over medium heat until tortilla on the bottom is golden brown. Flip over using two spatulas and heat other side until golden brown and cheese is melted, 2–3 minutes. Serve hot, cut into wedges, with light sour cream, salsa, or guacamole.

Variations: Fill with cooked lean ground beef, shredded cooked chicken, bits of ham, shredded zucchini, shredded carrot, and other shredded or chopped vegetables.

Vegetable oil spray
2 whole-wheat flour tortillas
1/4 cup combined cheddar and Monterey Jack cheese
2 slices bacon, cooked, drained, and crumbled
1 tablespoon chopped pitted black olives
1 tablespoon chopped mild green chilies

Porkies

4 turkey franks
4 hot dog buns
1 12-ounce can pork
    and beans or chili
    with beans
¼ cup shredded
    cheddar cheese

Add a little more good nutrition to an old favorite.

MAKES 4

Heat oven to 400°F. Cut a lengthwise slit down the middle of each frank without cutting all the way through. Place on hot dog bun and open up slit. Spoon beans into frank slit. Top with cheddar cheese. Wrap each bun in foil, twisting ends to seal. Bake for 20 minutes.

Turtles

It looks like a turtle, but it tastes like a hot dog!

MAKES 4

Split franks in half lengthwise. Melt margarine in a skillet, add franks, and cook until lightly browned. Spread relish on bottom halves of buns. Top with baked beans. Place two frank halves on top, forming an X. Cover with top halves of buns. Push carrot sticks into olives and insert sticks into rolls to form heads.

4 turkey franks
1 tablespoon margarine
¼ cup sweet pickle relish
4 hamburger rolls, split and toasted
1 cup baked beans, heated
4 carrot sticks
4 large pitted green or black olives

Wiener Pops

4 wooden skewers or
   ice cream sticks
4 turkey franks,
   heated
1 8-ounce jar cheese
   spread
¼ cup skim milk
1 cup crushed
   crackers, pretzels,
   or bread crumbs

Here are a couple of ways to serve your kids' favorites.

MAKES 4

Insert sticks in heated franks (or insert in franks and then heat them). In a saucepan, combine cheese and milk and heat until cheese melts, stirring constantly. Dip franks into cheese sauce, then roll in crushed crackers, pretzels, or bread crumbs.

Variation: Combine ¼ cup ketchup with ⅛ cup mustard. Roll franks in ketchup-mustard sauce, then roll in cracker crumbs, crushed pretzels, or bread crumbs.

Personalized Pizza

A pizza pie is a creative way to turn dinnertime into fun time. Use different vegetables and cheeses to make a monster face, a flower, or a greeting (spelled out in veggies) for your child.

SERVES 4–6

Heat oven to 400°F. Roll pizza dough into a round shape if crust is not premade. Pour pizza sauce over dough or crust. Top with a layer of mozzarella cheese. Make your child's face on top of the cheese by using tomatoes or pepperoni as eyes and cheeks, an olive or mushroom slice as a nose, red pepper slices as a mouth, and cheddar cheese as hair. Write your child's name at the bottom using the green bell pepper slices. Bake for 15–20 minutes, until cheese is melted and bubbly and crust is golden.

1 premade 16-ounce pizza crust or 10-ounce package pizza dough
1 10-ounce jar pizza sauce
1 cup shredded mozzarella cheese
2 cherry tomatoes, cut in half, or 4 pepperoni circles
1 olive or mushroom slice
3 slices red bell pepper
½ cup shredded cheddar cheese
1–2 green bell peppers, cut into thin slices

Cloud in a Cup

½ cup elbow macaroni
2 tablespoons
   chopped green bell
   pepper
1 tablespoon chopped
   onion
2 tablespoons
   margarine
4 teaspoons
   cornstarch
1 cup skim milk
1 cup shredded
   cheddar cheese
1 cup frozen corn
   kernels, thawed
2 eggs, separated
⅛ teaspoon cream of
   tartar

Whip up this light-as-a-cloud macaroni and cheese cup for dinner tonight.

MAKES 4

Heat oven to 350°F. Cook macaroni in boiling water according to package directions. Drain, rinse in cold water, and set aside. Cook green pepper and onion in margarine in a saucepan over medium heat until tender. Stir in cornstarch. Add milk and cook and stir until thickened and bubbly. Cook and stir for 2 more minutes. Reduce heat to low, add cheese and corn, and stir until cheese is melted. Remove from heat. Beat egg yolks lightly. Slowly add cheese mixture, stirring constantly. Fold macaroni into cheese mixture. Cool slightly. Wash and dry beaters, then beat egg whites and cream of tartar until stiff peaks form. Slowly fold beaten egg whites into cheese-macaroni mixture. Fill four ovenproof coffee mugs with egg mixture to within ¾ inch of tops. Place mugs on a baking sheet and bake for 25–30 minutes or until tops are golden brown.

Variation: Use different types of macaroni, such as wagon wheels or bow ties. Substitute peas for corn. Use a combination of cheddar and Monterey Jack cheeses.

Popeye Power Punches

2 tablespoons
   vegetable oil
1 small onion,
   chopped
1 pound lean ground
   beef
Garlic powder
1 bunch fresh
   spinach, cooked
1 cup grated cheddar
   cheese
12 small whole-wheat
   rolls

No need to tell the kids there's spinach in these Power Punches. Just let Popeye take over.

SERVES 4–6

Heat oven to 350°F. Heat oil in a skillet, add onion, and cook over medium heat until browned. Add beef and garlic powder to taste and simmer until meat is cooked through. Drain. Add spinach, mix well, then allow to cool. Cut off tops of rolls and hollow out middles. Add grated cheese to cooled mixture, then stuff into hollowed-out rolls. Replace tops. Wrap each in aluminum foil, then bake for 20 minutes.

Inside Out and Upside Down

Your little ones will love this good-for-you finger food.

SERVES 1

Wrap slice of mozzarella cheese around a soft bread stick and serve with a bowl of warm spaghetti sauce for dipping.

To lower fat: Choose lean meats and low-fat cheeses, yogurts, margarines, etc. Keep portions small. Broil, bake, or steam rather than fry. Trim fat from meat. Don't add a lot of extra fat, such as butter, sour cream, and so on. Read the labels on foods. Use skim milk and nonfat yogurt. Use vegetable oil spray to grease pans.

1 slice sliced
   mozzarella cheese
1 soft bread stick
¼ cup spaghetti
   sauce

Brer Rabbit Fondue

4 cups shredded
cheddar cheese
½ cup apple cider
1 tablespoon
cornstarch
½ teaspoon dry
mustard
⅛ teaspoon garlic
powder
1 teaspoon
Worcestershire
sauce
French bread, cut
into bite-size
pieces

We've taken the beer out of the rarebit and renamed this fun-to-eat fondue Brer Rabbit.

SERVES 4

In a saucepan over low heat, slowly heat cheese with all but 3 tablespoons of the apple cider. Mix cornstarch with the reserved cider, then slowly add to mixture along with mustard, garlic powder, and Worcestershire sauce. Stir until smooth. Pour into a fondue pot or bowl and serve with cut-up bread and fondue spears or forks for dipping.

Salad Cigar

Kids know that smoking is not good for them, but this portable Salad Cigar is great for their health.

MAKES 2

Rinse lettuce leaves and pat dry. Spread peanut butter on both leaves. Sprinkle on grated carrot, raisins, and seeds or nuts. Place a banana half at one side of leaf. Carefully roll up lettuce leaf around banana. Hold and eat.

2 head lettuce leaves
2 tablespoons peanut butter (creamy or chunky)
1 carrot, grated
2 tablespoons raisins
2 tablespoons sunflower seeds or chopped walnuts
1 banana, peeled and cut in half lengthwise

Attack of the Tasty Tarantulas

1 lettuce leaf
1 canned peach half
8 thin carrot sticks,
   2–3 inches long
2 raisins
½ cherry
2 cherry stems

Watch out—the tasty tarantulas are about to attack the dinner table. Your only defense is to gobble them up before they strike.

MAKES 1

Lay lettuce leaf on a small plate and set peach half, cut side down, in center of lettuce. Add raisin eyes, cherry mouth, cherry stem antennas, and carrot stick legs to form a tasty tarantula.

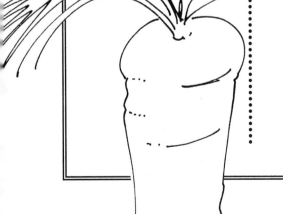

Funny Bunnies

Use your imagination to create different critters from different fruits. It's a great way to get the kids to eat salad.

MAKES 6

Place a lettuce leaf on each plate. Place one scoop cottage cheese on leaf for head. Place one pear half, cut side down, under cheese for body. Cut a second pear half lengthwise into 2 pieces and place above head to form ears. Cut each half slice of cheese into 6 narrow strips for whiskers and place 3 on each side of face. Use olive halves for eyes, cherry half for mouth, and dab of cottage cheese for tail.

6 lettuce leaves
1 16-ounce carton cottage cheese
2 16-ounce cans pear halves, drained
3 slices American cheese, cut in half
6 green olives stuffed with pimiento, cut in half
3 maraschino cherries, cut in half

207

Tweety Tweat

¼ cup cream cheese, softened
1 banana, peeled and cut in half crosswise
½ cup sunflower or sesame seeds or crushed cracker crumbs
6 raisins

This Tweety Tweat is sweet and really neat.

MAKES 2

Spread cream cheese on outside of both banana halves except on the cut end. Roll in seeds or crumbs. Poke in 2 raisins for eyes on each half. Flatten 2 raisins, cut in half, and stick 2 halves to cream cheese to form top and bottom of beak. Set both halves on a plate, cut sides down, so the birds stand up.

Variation: Turn this into Mickey Mouse by sticking pretzel halves into face to form whiskers and tail and using raisins to make eyes and nose and flattened raisins to make ears.

Diamond Mine

When a friend's daughter refused to eat her carrots, her mom smuggled them into the mashed potatoes and gave them a cute name. The little girl gobbled them right down. You might try some other vegetables instead of carrots.

SERVES 1–2

Prepare your favorite mashed potato recipe. When mashing, put in cooked carrots and mash them in with the potatoes. Serve to the kids and see if they can spot the "diamonds" in the pile of potatoes.

1 large or 2 medium potatoes
2–3 carrots, cooked

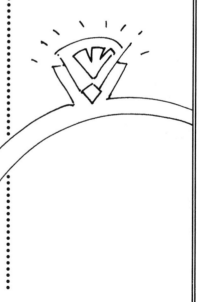

Goofy Garden Salad

1 cup grated carrot
1 cup chopped celery
1 cup chopped apple
½ cup raisins
½ cup chopped
   walnuts
2–3 tablespoons
   mayonnaise
1 teaspoon lemon
   juice

You can add and subtract whatever you want to put into your Goofy Garden Salad. But here's a basic foundation to begin with.

SERVES 4

Mix all ingredients well. Serve in a fun container such as a hollowed-out orange, cantaloupe half, or popover.

Variations: Add any of this goofy stuff:
   • Grated veggies
   • Chopped fruit
   • Chopped nuts
   • Seeds
   • Granola

Phony Pumpkins

Trick and treat the kids to these orange-corn muffins, made especially to go with your favorite dinner.

8 navel oranges
1 8-ounce box corn bread/muffin mix
Vegetable oil spray

MAKES 8

Heat oven to 400°F. Cut tops off oranges and scoop out pulp, being careful not to pierce orange rind. Prepare bread/muffin mix according to package directions. Lightly spray insides of orange shells with vegetable oil spray. Pour in muffin batter until shells are half full. Cover with orange lid, set in muffin tin or wrap in foil, and bake according to package directions, until golden brown on top. Draw face with permanent felt-tip pen on outside of orange and serve with a spoon or have the kids peel and eat.

Bread Stick Valentines

Vegetable oil spray
1 11-ounce can
   refrigerated bread
   stick dough
1 egg
1 tablespoon water
Poppy or sesame
   seeds (optional)

Bread sticks make great dinner side dishes and great craft materials. Let the kids make their own shapes or surprise them with your special creations. We like to make hearts, but you can shape your dough into anything—first-name initials, flowers, animals, unique designs, even monsters!

MAKES 8

Heat oven to 350°F. Spray a cookie sheet with vegetable oil spray. Separate dough into eight pieces. Twist or bend each piece into a heart shape or other design and place 2 inches apart on cookie sheet. Blend egg and water together and brush on dough. Add seeds if desired. Bake for 15 minutes, until golden brown.

Happy Face Pie

The Happy Face Pie comes out looking just like a frosted cake with a smile on it. But surprise—it's dinner!

SERVES 6–8

Heat oven to 350°F. Mix ground beef with zucchini and ketchup and press into a 9-inch round cake pan. Bake for 30–40 minutes. Remove from oven and pour off excess fat. Cover with whipped potatoes as if frosting a cake. Sprinkle shredded cheese around edge of pie to make hair and decorate with pickles, ketchup, and mustard to make a happy face.

1 pound lean ground beef
1 cup shredded zucchini
¼ cup ketchup
2 cups whipped potatoes
½ cup shredded cheddar cheese
2 pickles, sliced
Ketchup and mustard

7
Dazzling Desserts

Sunshine Balls

You can fill these creative containers with lots of tasty treats, but here's a favorite at our house.

4 oranges or lemons
1 quart fruit-flavored nonfat frozen yogurt
3 cups ice cubes

MAKES 4

Cut off tops of lemons or oranges and scoop out insides. Combine fruit with frozen yogurt and ice in a blender. Whirl until mixed. Scoop mixture into hollow shells, replace tops, and serve.

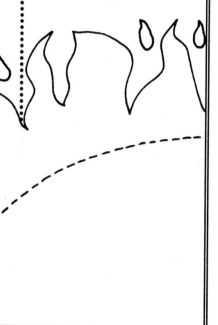

Upside-Down Sundaes

1 tablespoon chopped
   nuts
2 tablespoons nonfat
   whipped topping
1 tablespoon peanut
   butter (creamy or
   chunky), melted in
   microwave
1 tablespoon carob or
   chocolate syrup
2 tablespoons flaked
   coconut
1 scoop favorite flavor
   nonfat frozen
   yogurt, softened

For fun, have a backward day and do everything you can backward. For dessert, serve this Upside-Down Sundae.

MAKES 1

In a small individual serving dish, sprinkle a layer of chopped nuts. Next spoon out whipped topping so it covers bottom of bowl. Next drizzle on peanut butter and syrup. Then sprinkle on coconut. Finally, add 1 scoop frozen yogurt and spread it so it reaches all sides and is smooth. Serve.

Clown Face

The creative arrangement of fruit can turn a healthy and nutritious food into a fun-to-eat treat. Serve the Clown Face (or Puppy Dog variation) for dessert or use it as a snack or dinnertime salad.

1 canned pear half
1 carrot, shredded
2 raisins
1 maraschino cherry
1 slice red bell pepper
¼ cup cottage cheese

MAKES 1

Place pear half on plate with wide part at bottom and narrow part at top. Top with shredded carrot for hair, raisins for eyes, cherry for nose, bell pepper slice for mouth, and scoop cottage cheese at bottom for bow.

Variation: To make Puppy Dog, turn pear on its side, use plum half or prune for floppy ear, raisin for eye, cherry for nose, and cottage cheese at bottom for collar.

Porcupines

2 bananas, peeled
  and cut into
  fourths crosswise
¼ cup cream cheese,
  softened
Food coloring
½ cup flaked
  coconut, divided
  among 3–4 plastic
  sandwich bags
16 raisins

Porcupines are a colorful way to serve a fruity nutritious dessert.

SERVES 2

Spread bananas with soft cream cheese. Put 1–2 drops of food coloring into each bag of coconut, making each a different color. Drop cream cheese–covered bananas into bags and shake until coated. Set on a plate, add raisins as eyes, and serve.

Variation: Use creamy peanut butter instead of cream cheese and shredded carrot instead of coconut.

Banana Boats

An alternative to the ice cream version of the banana split.

MAKES 4

Wash bananas. Slit each one lengthwise with a sharp knife, cutting to within 1 inch of each end. Cut away ½ inch of the skin along each side of the slits with scissors. Pour cottage cheese, yogurt, or whipped topping into a bowl. Carefully scoop out insides of banana with a teaspoon, saving peels. Mix banana pieces with cottage cheese. Fill each peel with equal amounts of mixture. Sprinkle on chopped nuts and top with a cherry.

4 large bananas, unpeeled
½ cup low-fat cottage cheese, plain nonfat yogurt, or low-fat whipped topping
½ cup chopped peanuts
4 maraschino cherries, fresh cherries, or red grapes

Sunshine Island

1 orange
½ banana, peeled
2 strawberries
4 grapes
2 pitted dates
   (optional)
2 teaspoons flaked
   coconut
2 paper umbrellas
   (optional)

Shipwreck the kids on this sunny island filled with tropical fruit and fun.

MAKES 2

Cut orange in half and scoop out pulp. Cut up all fruit, mix well, and place in orange halves. Sprinkle with coconut and add a paper umbrella if desired.

Don't make desserts a reward for eating the rest of the meal. And don't use cookies and candies to make kids feel better physically or emotionally. This leads to eating disorders, and there are lots of other ways to make kids feel better, like hugs, stickers, and encouragement.

Grasshopper Pie

It's not really filled with grasshoppers, but it's crunchy and the kids will love the name.

Heat oven to 375°F. Spray a 9-inch pie pan with vegetable oil spray. Combine granola, 2 cups flour, and oil in a bowl and mix well. Add just enough fruit juice to form a soft dough. Divide mixture in half. Press into pie pan, covering bottom and sides. Toss fruit with remaining 1/4 cup flour, lemon juice, and cinnamon. Spoon into piecrust. Sprinkle on remaining granola mixture. Bake for 40 minutes, until fruit is soft. Cool and refrigerate.

Vegetable oil spray
1 cup granola cereal
2 1/4 cups flour
1/2 cup vegetable oil
1 tablespoon fruit juice
4 cups mixed fruit, such as apples, pears, peaches, pineapple, and berries, sliced as necessary
1 tablespoon lemon juice
1 teaspoon ground cinnamon

French Fancies

2 eggs, beaten
1 cup skim milk
1 cup flour
1/4 teaspoon ground
  cinnamon
Vegetable oil spray
2 cups cut-up fresh
  fruit

Crepes seem like such an elegant dessert, but they're really simple to make. Use whatever fruit is a family favorite.

MAKES 8

Stir together eggs, milk, flour, and cinnamon in a bowl. Spray a 6-inch skillet or crepe pan with vegetable oil spray and heat over medium heat. Pour in enough batter to cover the bottom of the pan and tilt pan to form a round crepe. Turn when lightly browned and cook on the other side. Remove from heat and fill with fresh fruit, raw or cooked, cold or warm.

Variations: Fill with nonfat frozen yogurt, fruit sauces, jam, nonfat whipped topping, applesauce, heated frozen fruit, or canned fruit filling.

Gorilla Bars

These carrot-stuffed brownies are full of good stuff, so let the kids monkey around with a handful after dinner.

MAKES 2 DOZEN

Heat oven to 350°F. Spray a 10" × 13" pan with vegetable oil spray. Melt margarine in a saucepan over medium heat. Add molasses and brown sugar and stir until sugar dissolves. Remove from heat and cool slightly. Beat eggs into margarine mixture. Stir in flours, oats, baking powder, and salt. Stir in carrot and walnuts. Pour into pan and bake for 25–30 minutes. Cool, cut into bars, and serve.

To store: These may be refrigerated in an airtight container for up to 1 week or frozen for up to 2 months.

Vegetable oil spray
½ cup margarine
⅓ cup molasses or honey
¼ cup packed brown sugar
2 eggs
½ cup whole-wheat flour
½ cup white flour
¼ cup rolled oats
2 teaspoons baking powder
¼ teaspoon salt
2 cups finely grated carrot
½ cup chopped walnuts

Berry-Good Bars

Vegetable oil spray
3/4 cup crushed
   pineapple in juice
1 egg
1/2 cup pineapple juice
1/4 teaspoon vanilla
   extract
1 tablespoon
   vegetable oil
1 1/2 cups flour
1 teaspoon baking
   soda
1 teaspoon baking
   powder
1/2 cup fresh
   blueberries

You can substitute strawberries, raspberries, or blackberries for the blueberries if desired.

MAKES 16 BARS

Heat oven to 350°F. Spray an 8-inch square pan with vegetable oil spray. Whirl 1/2 cup of the pineapple with juice in a blender until smooth. Beat together with egg, vanilla, and oil. Add flour, baking soda, and baking powder and beat well. Stir in blueberries and remaining pineapple. Pour into pan and bake for 20–25 minutes, until browned and a toothpick inserted in center comes out clean. Cool. Cut into squares.

To store: These may be refrigerated in an airtight container for up to 1 week or frozen for up to 2 months.

Johnny Appleseed Crumble

This tasty dessert covers three food groups and has more apples and oats than sugar.

SERVES 4–6

Heat oven to 350°F. Place apples in an 8-inch square pan sprayed with vegetable oil spray. Blend brown sugar, flour, oats, spices, and margarine together until crumbly. Spread over apples. Bake for 35 minutes, until topping is golden brown.

4 cups peeled, cored, and sliced baking apples (about 6 medium-size)
Vegetable oil spray
½ cup packed light brown sugar
½ cup flour
¾ cup rolled oats
¾ teaspoon ground cinnamon
¾ teaspoon ground nutmeg
⅓ cup margarine, cut into small pieces

Ooey-Gooey-Chewy Bars

Vegetable oil spray
1 8-ounce can pears
   in juice
2 eggs
⅓ cup vegetable oil
1½ cups flour
1 cup rolled oats
2 teaspoons baking
   powder
16 pitted dates
1–2 teaspoons water
   or fruit juice

The dates make them chewy; the chewing makes them ooey-gooey.

MAKES 16 BARS

Heat oven to 350°F. Spray two 8-inch square pans with vegetable oil spray. Whirl pears in a blender until smooth. Transfer to a bowl and beat in eggs and oil until creamy. Add flour, oats, and baking powder. Beat well. Divide mixture between pans and bake for 20 minutes, until browned and a toothpick inserted in center comes out clean. Turn out and cool. Blend dates in a blender until thick and pasty. Add enough water or juice to make mixture spreadable. Spread over one cake square, top with other cake square, and cut into bars.

To store: These may be refrigerated in an airtight container for up to 1 week or frozen for up to 2 months.

Increase fiber and starch: Serve bread, potatoes, rice, pasta, and unsweetened cereals. Look for whole grains and whole wheat. Serve fruits and vegetables unpeeled and raw. Offer plenty of liquids with fiber. Serve high-fiber foods such as oatmeal, brown rice, nuts and seeds, popcorn, dried beans, fruits and vegetables, whole-grain bread products.

Peter Rabbit's Cake

Vegetable oil spray
3 eggs
½ cup (1 stick)
   margarine,
   softened
1 cup pineapple juice
2½ cups flour
1 teaspoon baking
   soda
2 teaspoons baking
   powder
1 teaspoon ground
   cinnamon
3 cups grated carrot
1 cup well-drained
   crushed pineapple

Why do you think they call it Peter Rabbit's Cake?

SERVES 8–10

Heat oven to 350°F. Spray a 9″ × 13″ pan with vegetable oil spray. Beat together eggs, margarine, and pineapple juice in a bowl. Add flour, baking soda, baking powder, and cinnamon. Beat well. Stir in carrot. Spread in pan and sprinkle pineapple over batter. Bake for 30 minutes or until browned. Cool and serve.

To store: This may be refrigerated in an airtight container for up to 1 week.

Treasure Islands

Yo-ho-ho and a bowl of this yummy treasure makes a great adventure in eating for your little pirates.

SERVES 6

Heat oven to 400°F. Combine cherries, honey, and tapioca in a saucepan. Cook and stir over medium heat until bubbly. Stir in margarine. Pour into a 1½-quart casserole. Place biscuits over cherry mixture. Bake for 20 minutes, until a toothpick inserted in biscuit comes out clean.

4 cups fresh or frozen unsweetened pitted tart red cherries

⅓ cup honey

1 tablespoon quick-cooking tapioca

1 tablespoon margarine

6 refrigerator whole-wheat biscuits

Rainbow Gold

1 quart vanilla nonfat
frozen yogurt,
divided among
3 bowls
Yellow, red, and blue
food coloring
4 parfait glasses

A multicolored rainbow of layers with a pot
of gold at the bottom.

SERVES 4

One at a time, blend the three bowls of
frozen yogurt with one food coloring in a
blender just until yogurt is tinted and soft.
Place a layer of yellow yogurt in each
parfait glass. Then add a layer of blue and
finally a layer of red.

Peanut Butter Pudding

A smooth and satisfying way to end a healthy dinner.

SERVES 2

Combine all ingredients in a blender and whirl until smooth. Pour into individual serving dishes and refrigerate.

When the kids are sick, try to continue to serve them nutritious foods. Offer a variety that are easily tolerated and digested. Kids are usually more receptive to cold foods, such as frozen juice bars. Yogurt has lactobacillus, which helps kids with diarrhea.

1 banana, peeled and cut into chunks
½ cup plain nonfat yogurt
½ cup creamy peanut butter

Jack Horner's Plum Pudding

5 cups fresh, frozen,
   or canned pitted
   plums
3/8 cup cornstarch
Nonfat whipped
   topping

So quick and easy, it will make you feel guilty about whipping it up without work.

SERVES 4–6

Place plums in a blender and whirl until smooth. Add cornstarch and blend well. Pour into top of a double boiler. Cook over medium heat, stirring constantly, until it boils and thickens. Remove from heat, pour into custard cups, and refrigerate. Top with nonfat whipped topping if desired.

Cupid's Custard

Here's a light dessert to serve your loved ones after a big, hearty dinner.

SERVES 6

Heat oven to 350°F. Whirl ingredients in a blender until smooth. Pour into individual custard cups, sprinkle with a little more cinnamon, and place in large baking pan. Add hot water to a depth of 1 inch. Bake for 45 minutes, until custard is set and a toothpick inserted in center comes out clean. Cool and refrigerate until serving time.

1½ cups applesauce
1 cup skim milk
4 eggs
1 teaspoon ground cinnamon plus a little more for tops

Fire Bowls

1 3-ounce package
   sugar-free cherry,
   strawberry, or
   raspberry gelatin
¾ cup boiling water
1¾ cups applesauce
¼ teaspoon ground
   cinnamon

Fill their dessert cups with red-hot fun.

SERVES 4–6

Dissolve gelatin in boiling water according to package directions. Mix in applesauce and cinnamon. Pour into individual dessert cups and chill for 1 hour.

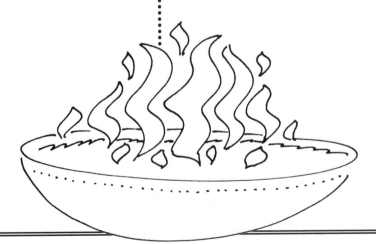

Orange Blossoms

You might want to add some tiny decorator flower candies to these bright and cheery Orange Blossoms.

SERVES 4–6

Dissolve gelatin in boiling water according to package directions. Add orange juice and stir in well. Add milk and stir in well. Pour into individual dessert cups. Chill for 1 hour.

1 3-ounce package sugar-free orange gelatin
¾ cup boiling water
1 cup orange juice
1 cup skim milk

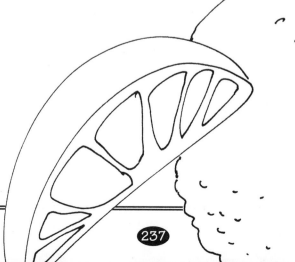

Caterpillars in Amber

Vegetable oil spray
1 3-ounce package
    yellow- or orange-
    colored sugar-free
    gelatin
1 cup boiling water
1 cup cold water
8 Gummi Worms or
    other Gummi
    insects

Take the kids back to prehistoric times, when dinosaurs roamed the earth and bugs were trapped in tree sap that turned to amber.

MAKES 8

Spray an 8-cup muffin tin with vegetable oil spray. Dissolve gelatin in boiling water according to package directions. Add cold water and mix well. Pour into muffin cups and place one Gummi Worm (we call them caterpillars) half in and half out of each muffin cup. Chill until firm, about 1 hour. Turn onto a large plate, then serve.

Variations:

• Fill cups with blue-colored gelatin, then drop Gummi Fishes into muffin cups to make Fish in the Sea.

• Use 3–4 colors of gelatin, such as red, orange, yellow, and green, and layer them in the muffin cups over a period of time. Turn onto plate to reveal Rainbow Cupcakes.

CONE HEADS

Kids think it's dessert when you serve them anything in an ice cream cone. Here are some suggestions:

Frozen yogurt • Cottage cheese • Applesauce • Fruit salad • Mashed banana • Cut-up Jell-O • Peanut butter mixed with cereal, raisins, and apple chunks

Monster Cookies

Vegetable oil spray
½ cup mashed
  banana
⅓ cup vegetable oil
¼ teaspoon vanilla
  extract
2 eggs
¼ cup skim milk
1¼ cups flour
¼ cup carob or
  sweetened cocoa
  powder
¼ teaspoon baking
  soda
1 cup chopped nuts or
  seeds
⅔ cup rolled oats

Monster Cookies for monster appetites. These have a rich brownie taste to satisfy that sweet tooth.

MAKES 4 DOZEN

Heat oven to 350°F and spray a cookie sheet with vegetable oil spray. Beat together banana, oil, vanilla, eggs, and milk in a bowl until creamy. Add flour, carob powder, and baking soda; beat well. Stir in chopped nuts or seeds and rolled oats. Mix well. Drop by large serving spoons onto cookie sheet to make giant cookies. Bake for 10–12 minutes, until just firm to the touch. Cool and serve.

To store: These may be refrigerated in an airtight container for up to 1 week or frozen for up to 2 months.

Peanut Butter Buddies

Spread a little jelly over these peanut butter cookies for a familiar taste combination.

MAKES 2 DOZEN

Heat oven to 375°F. Spray a cookie sheet with vegetable oil spray. Beat together banana, peanut butter, eggs, vanilla, and margarine in a bowl until creamy. Add flour and baking powder and mix well. Stir in chopped peanuts. Drop by teaspoonfuls onto cookie sheet. Press fork in center to make stripe pattern. Top with a whole peanut in center. Bake for 6–8 minutes or until lightly browned. Cool and serve.

To store: These may be refrigerated in an airtight container for up to 1 week or frozen for up to 2 months.

Vegetable oil spray
1/4 cup mashed
   banana
1/2 cup peanut butter
   (creamy or chunky)
2 eggs
3/4 teaspoon vanilla
   extract
2 tablespoons
   margarine,
   softened
1 cup flour
1/2 teaspoon baking
   powder
1 cup chopped
   peanuts
24 whole shelled
   peanuts

Full Moon Cookies

Vegetable oil spray
4 eggs
½ cup vegetable oil
1 6-ounce can frozen
   pineapple juice
⅓ cup lemon juice
2 cups flour
½ teaspoon baking
   powder

Sweet and tangy cakelike cookies to serve after a full meal.

MAKES 4 DOZEN

Heat oven to 375°F. Spray a cookie sheet with vegetable oil spray. Beat together eggs, oil, pineapple juice concentrate, and lemon juice. Add flour and baking powder; beat well. Drop by teaspoonfuls onto cookie sheet and bake for 8–10 minutes, until cookies are raised and firm to the touch and bottoms are lightly browned. Cool and serve.

Variations: Substitute frozen orange juice concentrate or apple juice concentrate for pineapple.

To store: These may be refrigerated in an airtight container for up to 1 week or frozen for up to 2 months.

Birthday parties are a tough time to keep up the good nutrition work. But with a little creativity you can offer a festive party with healthy foods. First, serve the kids a healthy snack to fill their tummies with good nutrition. When it's time to serve cake and ice cream, why not offer them a carrot cake and nonfat frozen yogurt? Send them home with trail mix instead of candy.

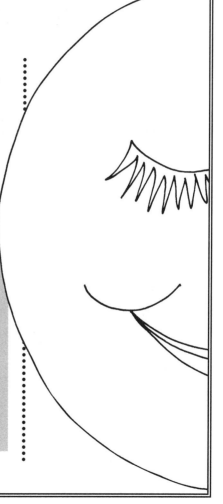

Peanut Butter Marbles

½ cup peanut butter
   (creamy or chunky)
¼ cup evaporated
   milk
¼ cup packed light
   brown sugar
1 teaspoon ground
   cinnamon
1 cup crispy chow
   mein noodles,
   slightly crushed
1 cup bite-size
   shredded wheat
   cereal, slightly
   crushed
¼ cup chopped
   peanuts
¼ cup raisins or
   currants

The kids could play a game of marbles with these, but they just won't last long enough!

MAKES 2 DOZEN

Combine peanut butter, evaporated milk, brown sugar, and cinnamon in a saucepan. Cook and stir over medium heat for 5 minutes. Remove and stir in noodles, shredded wheat, peanuts, and raisins. Drop by rounded teaspoonfuls onto a wax paper–lined cookie sheet. Chill for 1 hour.

To store: These may be refrigerated in an airtight container for up to 1 week or frozen for up to 2 months.

Magic Minimountains

These little boulders are full of crunch and make a great after-dinner cookie.

MAKES 2 DOZEN

Combine cereal, cracker crumbs, apricots, nuts, and peanut butter in a bowl. Stir in corn syrup and orange juice. With buttered hands, shape into balls. Chill before serving.

To store: These may be refrigerated in an airtight container for up to 1 week or frozen for up to 2 months.

½ cup Grape-Nuts cereal
½ cup crushed graham crackers
½ cup chopped dried apricots
½ cup chopped pecans
½ cup peanut butter (creamy or chunky)
¼ cup light corn syrup
1 tablespoon orange juice or water

Buttons, Buttons

Vegetable oil spray
3/4 cup sunflower
   seeds
1/4 cup rolled oats
1 banana, peeled
1 egg
1 tablespoon oil
2 tablespoons honey
48 raisins

Buttons, buttons, who's got the buttons?
The kids, of course.

MAKES 2 DOZEN

Heat oven to 350°F. Spray a cookie sheet
with vegetable oil spray. Whirl sunflower
seeds and oats in a blender until finely
ground. Mash banana with a fork. Mix
together all ingredients except raisins in a
bowl. Drop by rounded teaspoonfuls onto
cookie sheet and place two raisins in
center of each to make button eyes. Bake
for 15–20 minutes, until lightly browned on
the bottom. Cool and serve.

To store: These may be refrigerated in an
airtight container for up to 1 week or
frozen for up to 2 months.

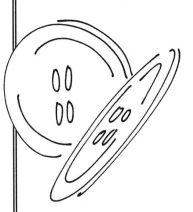

Strawberry Cracker Crunchies

Let the kids help you make these creamy, crunchy crackers.

1 cup fresh or frozen
   strawberries
½ cup cream cheese,
   softened
12 graham crackers

MAKES 1 DOZEN

Blend strawberries in a blender until smooth. Add cream cheese and whirl until creamy and smooth. Spread strawberry-cream cheese mixture on crackers and serve.

Worms in the Dirt

1 plastic flowerpot,
    about 6" tall × 4"
    wide
1 pint chocolate
    nonfat frozen
    yogurt, softened
1 10-ounce package
    chocolate wafer
    cookies, crushed
4–6 Gummi Worms
1 plastic flower with
    stem

Kids and dirt seem to go together like peanut butter and jelly. Toss in a couple of worms and you have a crazy dessert the kids will love to sink their teeth into.

SERVES 6

Clean flowerpot and line with foil. Fill with softened frozen yogurt to within about 1½ inches from top. Cover with a layer of crushed cookies. Stick in a few Gummi Worms and freeze until serving time. When it's time to eat, remove from freezer, stick in plastic flower, and set on the table with bowls. Watch the kids' reaction as you start serving dessert from the flowerpot.

Index

255